SUNDAY'S SCRIPTURES
An Interpretation

William Sydnor

Rector
Christ Church
Alexandria, Virginia

Book cover design by Frankie Welch

MOREHOUSE-BARLOW CO., INC.
WILTON, CONNECTICUT

With love and graditude

to Caroline

and those beautiful people

Gleaves

Carrie

Sarah

Jeannie

Buck

Copyright © 1976

Morehouse-Barlow Co., Inc.
'78 Danbury Road, Wilton, Ct. 06897

ISBN 0-8192-1215-6

Printed in the United States of America

CONTENTS

Preface

The progenitor of this book is my *How and What the Church Teaches* (New York, Longmans, Green and Co., 1960), which came about because of a compulsion to help people understand those portions of Scripture they were hearing in church. This has been a concern of religious leaders in the Biblical tradition since at least the days of Ezra (Neh. 8:2-10).

My earlier book was intended primarily for parish priests and Sunday school teachers. It gave the clergyman a quick glance at Sunday's Scripture, which proved helpful in sermon preparation and in whatever brief oral introduction might precede Scripture reading in a service. Sunday school teachers found it valuable in preparing next week's lesson. But the book took on wider uses than anticipated. The explanations were printed in Sunday church bulletins, like program notes at a concert, to help the congregation appreciate what they were hearing. And parish priests were putting it in the hands of their layreaders. Some parishes actually used the book as a parish-wide home study book. Parish families read the lections during the week prior to the appointed Sunday and talked about their meaning; then came to church on Sunday to listen intelligently to the Scripture—and the sermon.

It is my hope that this book will fill those same needs and, please God, others as well. For the lectionary (and here, specifically, the Episcopal Church lectionary of 1976) has entered upon a new day. It has been liturgical interest and practice throughout Christendom. Significant work has been done on the lectionary by scholars of a number of churches: Roman Catholic, Lutheran, Presbyterian, and others. Their work has been studied and taken into account in the preparation of the new Episcopal lectionary of 1976. And they in turn will be examining ours in the same way. Because of this, there is reason to hope that this book will have value to Christians who have no connection with the Episcopal Church.

My chief indebtedness is to my colleagues on the sub-committee of the Standing Liturgical Commission of the Episcopal Church with whom I worked in preparing this lectionary: the Rev. Reginald H. Fuller and the Rev. Frank R. VanDevelder, both professors at Virginia Theological Seminary, Alexandria, Va. Dr. Fuller is also author of a book on the lectionary. The other member of the committee was Captain Howard Galley, C.A., Editorial Assistant to the Liturgical Commission's Coordinator for Prayer Book Revision. Captain Galley has also been most accommodating in making available to me last-minute copies of lectionary material which will be published in the proposed revision of the Prayer Book to be considered by General Convention in 1976. The insights of these four gentlemen should be footnoted on every page of the Introduction.

The Rev. Charles P. Price, a member of the Standing Liturgical Commission and also a professor at Virginia Seminary, generously took time to read and criticize the Introduction. This criticism was wonderfully helpful.

I am grateful to Mrs. Marilyn Anderson, who typed the manuscript, and to Miss Caroline Tillotson, for whose editorial skill I am deeply indebted. But most of all I am thankful for my wife, Caroline, who understands the discipline required of one who is writing a book.

William Sydnor

Alexandria, Virginia.
December 27, 1975

Introduction

The Lectionary is not static. It is revised more often than the text of the Prayer Book itself. But in the past this has usually been a change in details—different chapters and verses, or readings selected to provide more stories or more emphasis on evangelical outreach or apocalyptic or judgment or whatever. The new lectionary of 1976 has a completely changed point of view. The whole rationale has been rethought. As the sportscaster would say, "It's a whole new ball game." Here then is what one needs to know to understand and use this lectionary to best advantage.

The Basis of Unity

In the past, the appointed Scripture was generally (but not always) related to the Collect for the Day. Like many other parish priests I taught my people that the collect drew together in a prayer the thought of the day; it was the collecting prayer. I felt the sermon was appropriate for the day when the lections illustrated its points and the day's collect was the appropriate prayer with which to close. Not any more. Save on the great feasts, the collect only by sheer coincidence touches on the theme of the day.

Now the basis for unity is the Gospel. This is true in the broadest and most profound sense. It is not just the determining factor in the unity of the service. Its use is a symbol of the unity of Christendom. For the passage used is also the appointed Gospel on the same day of a major part of Christendom in the United States and Canada and even beyond. This widespread use across denominational lines began in 1969 with the publication of the Roman Catholic *Ordo Lectionum Missae*. Here is what Eugene L. Brand, Division for Parish Services, the Lutheran Church in America, has written regarding the ripple effect of the appearance of that document:*

> Publication of this lectionary has had a far-reaching ecumenical impact, especially in North America. Both because of the sweep of its concept and the thoroughness of its scholarship, it commended itself to other churches. The Presbyterian *Worshipbook* (1970) and the *Services for Trial Use* (1971) of the Episcopal Church both contain lectionaries based upon it. *The Church Year—Calendar and*

*Reginald H. Fuller, *Preaching the New Lectionary: the Word of God for the Church Today* (Collegeville, Minnesota: The Liturgical Press, 1971-1974), xiv-xv.

Lectionary (1973) of the Inter-Lutheran Commission on Worship follows a similar course. The United Church of Christ and the Christian Church (Disciples of Christ) have adopted the Presbyterian revision, and the Commission on Worship of the Consultation on Church Union prepared a revision to which the Methodist Church is committed.

In a few short years virtually all American and Canadian churches will be using lectionaries more notable for their similarities than for their differences. . .it is thrilling to contemplate the sign of Christian unity as the churches of our Lord order their worship according to the same portions of Scripture and base their proclamation of God's Good News on the same blessed words.

For a long time we have been singing "The Church's one foundation/Is Jesus Christ her Lord." For a long time we have been saying the same Creed. For a long time we have recognized as valid baptism with water in the Name of the Holy Trinity. So our commitment to "one Lord, one faith, one baptism, one God and Father of us all" (Eph. 4:5-6), which has long been a theological truth, is now ecumenically obvious in our worship. Now the order of service (because of the revisions in sequence in the Eucharist) and the content of the service (because of this lectionary) make it evident that the Lord's Table around which we gather is truly *his,* and our worship is no longer so denominationally precious and exclusive that others feel like outsiders. Our Lord prayed that his followers "may be one even as we are one" (Jn. 17:11). In the 1950's and 1960's a strong effort was made by representative church leaders around a conference table to find a basis for organic unity embracing a number of Christian bodies. The ecumenical thrust of the 1970's is that rank and file members of the Christian Church find their common life in gathering around the Lord's Table.

The Plan of the Lectionary

For each Sunday there are three appointed readings plus an appropriate psalm or psalms or portions thereof. The first reading is from the Old Testament, the second is the Epistle, and the third is the Gospel passage. At Morning and Evening Prayer the second reading may be either of the New Testament passages.

The first consideration of the Lectionary Sub-Committee in selecting the readings was ecumenical. What is the passage appointed to be read on this occasion by the Roman Catholics, the Lutherans, the Presbyterians, *et al*? (Incidently, these other churches were—and are—equally influenced by our selections.) In the present lectionary, the Gospel is with rare exceptions the same as that appointed for use by our brethren in the other churches. The Epistle is often the same. The Old Testament lesson is usually our own choice and rarely corresponds (with the exception of Lent), and the psalm is for the most part the same as the others are using.

a) *The Gospel*

The lectionary is laid out in a three-year cycle. In Year A (which always begins on Advent Sunday in years divisible by three) Matthew's Gospel is read almost in its entirety. In Year B Mark is read, and in Year C Luke. Portions of the Fourth Gospel are read in all three years on the great feasts, during Holy Week, and in the Easter season. As we said, the central thought of the appointed lections is usually taken from the Gospel of the Day.

b) *The Epistle*

"The Epistles are not supposed to be related to the Old Testament or the Gospel," explains Dr. Reginald Fuller, a member of the Sub-committee on the Lectionary of the Standing Liturgical Commission. The obvious reason why this is so is that both the Epistle and the Gospel from which the appointed passages are taken are being read serially Sunday by Sunday. Only by merest chance is there any likelihood of their being on the same theme. There are, however, several exceptions to this pattern. On the three great feast days of Christmas, Easter, and Pentecost, the Epistle is related to the theme of the occasion. And during the seasons of Advent and Lent the Epistle is integrated into the meaning of the season. On the First Sunday of Advent the theme is eschatological, looking to Christ's second coming. On the Second and Third Sundays the ministry of John the Baptist is central, and on the Fourth Sunday the annunciation is the theme. The Epistles have been chosen to fit into this pattern. During Lent the Epistles deal with the believers' participation in the death and resurrection of Jesus in baptism and in the Christian life. Or to put it another way, the Epistles are either explanations of the meaning of the cross or of the believers' participation in salvation through baptism.*

c) *Old Testament Readings*

Most of the time the Old Testament readings relate to the appointed Gospel. But in Lent the Old Testament is pivotal because it is a sequential dealing with God's mighty acts. The Epistle and/or the Gospel relate to it. The Standing Liturgical Commission explains the matter in this way: "The proper of the season returns to the ancient emphasis upon a synopsis of the history of the salvation of the Old Testament, and the signs in Jesus' ministry that point to his death and resurrection. These are all gathered

---

*Reginald H. Fuller, *Preaching the New Lectionary: the Word of God for the Church Today* (Collegeville, Minn.: The Liturgical Press, 1971-74), pp.148, 332.

together in the great Vigil Service of Easter Eve."*

The Book of Acts is intended to be read during the Easter Season each year instead of an Old Testament reading. However, Old Testament passages have been provided as alternatives.

The Psalms

The appointed psalter is likely to correspond to that used in the Roman Catholic and other lectionaries. It has been selected because of verses or phrases which echo the central thought of the day. The meaning of a given psalm in its entirety is not the major consideration.

There is a suggested edited shortening of the psalm for those who prefer a shorter version to use as a gradual reading at the Eucharist. All psalm references are from the 1976 version of the Psalter. Therefore, the verse references may differ from the 1928 Prayer Book version.

The Propers Rubric

Formerly, in order to accommodate the fact that Easter might occur on any of thirty-five days in March and April, the Trinity season either added one or more propers from late Epiphany or lopped off a late Trinity Sunday or two. Now, in order to bring the Episcopal Church into line with other branches of Christendom, the accommodation is at the beginning rather than the end of the Pentecost season. Here is the rubric which explains how that will take place:

> The Proper to be used on each of the Sundays after Pentecost (except for Trinity Sunday) is determined by the calendar date of that Sunday. Thus, in any year, the Proper for the Sunday after Trinity Sunday is the numbered Proper (number 3 through number 8), the calendar date of which falls on that Sunday or is closest to it, whether before or after. Thereafter, the Propers are used consecutively. For example, if the Sunday after Trinity is May 26, the sequence begins with Proper 3 (Propers 1 and 2 being available for use on the weekdays of Pentecost and Trinity weeks). If the Sunday after Trinity Sunday is June 13, the sequence begins with Proper 6 (Propers 1 through 3 being omitted that year, and Propers 4 and 5 being available for use in Pentecost and Trinity weeks).**

*The Church Year, Prayer Book Studies 19 (New York, The Church Hymnal Corp., 1970), 27.

**The Draft Proposed Book of Common Prayer (New York; The Church Pension Fund Corp.), p.158.

On the weekdays following the Feast of Pentecost we are directed to use the numbered Proper which most closely corresponds to the date of Pentecost, and on the weekdays following Trinity Sunday we are directed to use the numbered Proper which most closely corresponds to the date of Trinity Sunday.

There are several advantages of this new method of determining the propers for this longest season of the Church year. Two stand out. First, an increasingly large proportion of Christendom will now be using the same propers on the same Sunday during the entire year and not just during the first half of it. Another advantage is that now the Church year, which began by highlighting our anticipation of the celebration of Christ's coming down from heaven, will also on its closing Sundays emphasize our anticipation that he will come again to judge the living and the dead. This eschatological theme of the last Sundays of the year leads smoothly into the First Sunday of Advent, when we become aware that he whose nativity we are beginning to prepare for is also he who will come to be our Judge.

Do not worry if the above rubric seems involved and complicated. (It seems that way to me, too.) In the explanations of the propers later in this book all you need to know in order to stay on the track is the date on the calendar.

Some Needed Explanations

There is a liberal use of parentheses in the Biblical references. If you want to read a short lection, ignore the parenthetic verses, for example, in A Lent 4: John 9:1-13, 28-38. If you prefer to read a longer version, include the parenthetic verses in your reading: John 9:1-13 (14-27) 28-38. But in any case list in the church bulletin the passage which the congregation will hear, with no parentheses: John 9:1-38.

All the Biblical citations are from the Revised Standard Version. Sometimes it has seemed appropriate to begin the reading with the second half of the verse—for example, in A Proper 7, Romans 5:15b-19; or to end a reading or a section thereof with only the first half of a verse—for example, in A Proper 4, Romans 3:21-25a, 28. *Caution:* If part of a verse is indicated, be sure to use the Revised Standard Version.

The opening verse of the appointed reading may not be intelligible to members of the congregation who are not hearing it in the context of the whole passage. To avoid this difficulty two kinds of opening verses need to be watched for especially. (1) Does the opening verse contain a pronoun which refers to a person or place mentioned earlier in the text? For example, the I Kings 19:9-18 reading (B Last Sunday after the Epiphany) begins, "And there he came to a cave, and lodged there; and behold, the word of the Lord came to him. . . ." Who is he and where is he? Provide this information with an edited lead-in opening verse: "*On Horeb, the mount of God, Elijah* came to a cave, and lodged there; and behold, the word of the Lord came to him. . . ." (2) If the opening verse is a direct quotation, indicate who is speaking. For example, the Hosea 2:14-23 reading (B Epiphany 8) opens with, "Therefore, behold, I will allure her. . . ." It is more intelligible to begin, "*Thus says the Lord,* 'Therefore, behold, I will allure her. . . .' " Or *Jesus said*, 'Let not your hearts be troubled. . . .' " (John 14:1-14, A Easter 5). The reader needs to put himself in the place of his hearers and do what he can to make the passage intelligible. Most lead-ins are suggested in the material which follows, but the person who is to read at a service should always be alert to the need to supply such help for his hearers.

Finally, the explanatory material printed in the church bulletin or told to the congregation should not be cluttered with footnotes. However, the person who wishes to know where a quotation comes from or where he can pursue some explanation more extensively deserves that information. For this reason there are occasional references of the briefest sort. (But even these should not appear in a church bulletin reprint.) Here are the books to which these parenthetic references refer. The reference will always be found in that book's discussion of the passage or verse in question.

J.C. Fenton: *The Gospel of St. Matthew* (Baltimore, Penguin Books, 1963).

D.E. Nineham: *The Gospel of St. Mark* (Baltimore, Penguin Books, 1963).

G.B. Caird: *The Gospel of St. Luke* (Baltimore, Penguin Books, 1963).

John Marsh: *The Gospel of St. John* (Baltimore, Penguin Books, 1968).

The Interpreter's Bible (Nashville, Abingdon-Cokesbury Press, 1951-1957), I-XII.

Arthur Weiser: *The Psalms—A Commentary* (Philadelphia, Westminister Press, 1962).

The Sunday Lectionary

Year A

Advent

First Sunday of Advent

Theme: God will judge his people.

Psalm 122

This is a pilgrim song which was sung just as they arrived at Jerusalem or, more likely, just as they were leaving on their journey. Its appropriateness on this day lies in the words, "For there are the thrones on judgment" (v.5).

Isaiah 2:1-5

In one of the opening oracles of his book, the prophet foresaw the day when God would judge his people. Consequently, he urges, "Come, let us walk in the light of the Lord."

Romans 13:8-14

Salvation (which includes judgment) is very near. The apostle urges that his readers cast off the works of darkness and keep the law. The accent is on the spirit with which we treat others rather than on nit-picking compliance with details of the legal code.

Matthew 24:37-44

The Lord's coming which we celebrate at Christmas is twofold: the nativity, a historical event, and his second coming, an eschatological event. This reading, like all of Matthew 24-25, is about that day at the end of history when Christ, the eternal Judge, will pass judgment on all of us and what we have done individually and corporately.

(Lead in: *"On the Mount of Olives, Jesus said to his disciples privately. . ."*)

Second Sunday of Advent

Theme: The coming Messiah will bring judgment and justice.

Psalm 72 [at the Eucharist: vss. 1-8]

This psalm has been interpreted by some scholars as referring to the Messiah. He will deliver the poor, the oppressed, the needy, the persecuted.

This is in the mainstream of Old Testament expectations of the coming of the Messiah.

Isaiah 11:1-10
The prophet describes poetically the coming messianic age when the Son of David ("root of Jesse"), God's appointed deliverer of his people, arrives. He foresees judgment and the administration of justice. He also foresees brotherhood and deep concern for others. This description of the lot of the faithful is a companion piece with the description of the judgment that will befall the wicked (Isa. 13:6-13). The latter lies behind the ominous preaching of John the Baptist.

Romans 15:4-13
When we consider the sin, suffering, and distress throughout the world and in our own lives, we are understandably dismayed and discouraged. Today's Old Testament reading says that God will send his own deliverer, and the Gospel reading tells us to prepare to receive him. In the light of Scripture passages such as these, the apostle appropriately closes his ethical section (chaps. 12-15) with a prayer that we may find joy and peace in believing.

Matthew 3:1-12
This is the account of the preaching of John the Baptist, which was the prelude to the ministry of Jesus (Mal. 4:5-6 and Mt. 11:13-15; 17:10-13). Here is a serious warning in preparation for the coming of the Messiah.

Third Sunday of Advent

A

Theme: The Lord will come with saving power and judgment.

Psalm 146 [at the Eucharist vss. 4-9]
The list of reasons why the psalmist can sing such exultant praise to God reads like a description of Jesus' ministry: "justice to the oppressed," "food to the hungry," "opens the eyes of the blind," "cares for the stranger. . . the fatherless and widow."

Isaiah 35:1-10
The prophet foretells the coming day of the Lord, when his glory will be revealed and his will done on earth as it is in heaven. Note that salvation and judgment are integral to the glory of the Lord which is to be revealed.

James 5:7-10
In this bit of early Christian writing, it is evident that the author believes that the Lord will soon come as the righteous Judge, and that his coming is

best prepared for by accepting with patient steadfastness whatever suffering is our lot.

Matthew 11:2-11
Jesus enumerates for John the Baptist's followers evidences that the promised Messiah has come. His words lean heavily on Isaiah 35. Frequently we see how steeped Jesus was in O.T. Scriptures. Note that he considered John the connecting link between the old order and the new.

Fourth Sunday of Advent

Theme: The Lord is at hand. A

Psalm 24 [at the Eucharist vss. 1-7]
This liturgical psalm is appropriate on the eve of Christmas. It exhorts us to live lives which will "receive a blessing from the Lord" and then heralds the imminent arrival of the King of glory.

Isaiah 7:10-17
Scholars consider this one of the Bible's most difficult passages to explain. Isaiah was a member of the court of Ahaz, King of Judah. The prophet's advice on a proposed international alliance is coupled with a message of doom because of Ahaz's unfaithfulness to the Lord. The passage is read today because it has become identified with the birth of Jesus.

Romans 1:1-7
The opening words of Paul's epistle introduce us to Jesus Christ—who he is and the blessings which are ours because of him.

Matthew 1:18-25
This account of the birth of Jesus contains a quotation from today's Isaiah reading. The fact that it is an inaccurate translation of the Hebrew text does not in any way detract from the beauty of this tender story.

Christmas Day, First Proper

A

Theme: Christ the Savior is born.

Psalm 96 [at the Eucharist: vss, 1-4, 11-12]
For the Christian, almost every verse of this psalm has to do with the Savior's birth.

Isaiah 9:2-4, 6-7

The prophet wrote this poem about the Messiah who was to come. It is impossible to read it without seeing in it a full-blown description of our Lord and his mission.

Titus 2:11-14

This epistle was written perhaps one hundred years after the crucifixion-resurrection. It contains practical advice to leaders of the early Church. This section is particularly appropriate on Christmas Day.

Luke 2:1-14 [15-20]

This wonderful prose-poetry gives us an unforgettable picture of the nativity. The angel's announcement is for all time the classic statement of the Good News.

Christmas Day, Second Proper

A

Theme: Christ the Lord has come.

Psalm 97 [at the Eucharist: vss. 1-2, 8-12]

The special character of this psalm "allows an insight into the depth and comprehension of the O.T. idea of the kingdom of God" (Weiser). This is appropriate at the celebration of the birth of him who ushered in that kingdom.

Isaiah 62:6-7, 10-12

Chapter 62 describes in a poem the people of God, the messianic people. In the first of the two stanzas we hear, the people are in tiptoe expectancy. The second depicts that people when the Messiah (Greek, *Christ*) has come. Here is the source of our Christmas joy.

Titus 3:4-7

This advice to early Christian leaders becomes an appropriate sermonette when we hear it on this day.

(Lead in: *"When the goodness and loving kindness of God. . ."*)

Luke 2:[1-14], 15-20

Our whole Biblical memory of Christmas centers in the angelic announcement to the shepherds and their visit to the manger Babe.

Christmas Day, Third Proper

A

Theme: The Word has become flesh and dwells among us.

Psalm 98 [at the Eucharist: vss. 1-6]

The coming of Jesus Christ gives the "new song" of the psalmist deeper significance than he dreamed of. All creation is exhorted (vss. 7-9), along with God's people to sing of the marvelous things God has done (v.1).

Isaiah 52:7-10

These glorious verses are from a poem which might be entitled "The Lord Has Become King" (51:17-52:12). Here the arrival of the bearer of good news and the effect of his proclamation are described in unforgettable words.

Hebrews 1:1-12

This first chapter of Hebrews describes the incarnation of God's Son in terms of its eternal significance.

John 1:1-14

Like Hebrews, the Fourth Gospel describes the coming of God's Son from the point of view of God's eternal purpose and of man's response. The meaning of "Word" is pivotal. It embraces God's creative power, his purpose, his wisdom and providence.

First Sunday after Christmas

A

Theme: God's grace is manifested in Jesus Christ.

Psalm 147 [at the Eucharist: vss. 13-21]

This psalm contains the essence of Hebrew worship. God is praised because of his power and because of "his compassionate grace as manifested in creation and election " (Weiser). But with the coming of Jesus Christ, God's grace has been set in a higher key (Jn. 1:16-17).

Isaiah 61:10-62:3

In some of the most stirring poetry of the Bible an ancient seer sings of the glad tidings of salvation to Zion. Heard on this day, these words become part of the profound joy of the feast of Christ's nativity.

Galatians 3:23-25; 4:4-7

With the coming of Christ, man's relation to God has changed radically from legalism to faith. Paul explains that the discipline of trying to keep the law was the training that prepares us for faith in Christ's merciful power. The emphasis has changed from seeking to gain God's favor by the good works we do to putting our faith in his love for us. It is the difference between a slave and an adopted son.

John 1:1-18

The Prologue of John's Gospel also makes clear the point of the Galatians passage above. "The law was given through Moses; grace and truth came through Jesus Christ" (v.17). "Grace" here means undeserved, unexpected kindness and caring.

Holy Name, January 1

A

Theme: Hallowed by thy Name.

Psalm 8

In the refrain with which this psalm opens and closes, God's name is the revelation of his nature. The intervening verses expand on this, ringing with fear and joy, thus blending the two opposite fundamental religious attitudes.

Exodus 34:1-8

Moses, in a rage at the people's apostasy, had broken the tablets on which the Ten Commandments were written (Exod. 32:19). Now he goes up the mountain a second time to receive the Commandments from God. In the encounter with God, Moses proclaims the Name of the Lord in the words of the old liturgical confession which is often repeated throughout the O.T. (II Chron. 30:9; Neh. 9:17,31; Joel 2:13; Jonah 4:2; Ps. 86:15; etc.). (Note: In v.5 most commentators designate Moses as the subject of the verb "stood." The reading becomes clearer if this is done.)

Romans 1:1-7

The salutation with which Paul's epistle opens indicates the motive which inspired his mission. Through Jesus Christ our Lord we have received grace (power) and apostleship to bring about obedience to the faith for the sake of his name among all the nations (v.5).

Alternate Epistle: Philippians 2:9-13

This is the latter part of Paul's almost lyrical description of the meaning of the incarnation. Because he who came from God died and rose again for us, his Name is revered in this world and beyond, and he is acknowledged as Lord by "every tongue."

Luke 2:15-21

This is the account of the naming of Jesus in the nativity story. The name Jesus means "Yahweh is salvation." He was given that name because "he will save his people from their sins" (Mt. 1:21).

Second Sunday after Christmas

A

Theme: The Lord's pilgrims

Psalm 84 [at the Eucharist: vss. 1-8]
   This is a pilgrim song. "Happy are the people. . . whose hearts are set on the pilgrims' way" (v.4). This could once have been sung by the Holy Family as they journeyed to the feast at Jerusalem or, in essence, been the sentiment of the Wise Men as they journeyed.

Jeremiah 31:7-14
   Within Jeremiah's book is a little Book of Comfort (chaps. 30-31). This portion of it describes in a poem the return to Zion of exiles from all nations. Here is the joy of pilgrims whose anticipation is soon to be realized.

Ephesians 1:3-6, 15-19a
   The writer begins his epistle with the thanksgiving for the receipt of "every spiritual blessing in the heavenly places" (v.3) by the Ephesians, whom he describes as "having the eyes of your hearts enlightened" (v.18). They had made a spiritual pilgrimage.

Matthew 2:13-15. 19-23
   This is the account of the flight of the Holy Family into Egypt to avoid the wrath of King Herod, and of their ultimate return to Galilee and the city of Nazareth, where Jesus grew up.
   (Lead in: *"Now when the wise men had departed. . . ."*)

Alternate Gospel: Luke 2:41-52
   The only boyhood story about Jesus is this account of what happened when he and his family made the pilgrimage to Jerusalem at Passover time.

Alternate Gospel: Matthew 2:1-12
   The story of the Wise Men coming to worship the Christ Child is a beloved part of the Christmas sequence. The major theme of Matthew's Gospel is that the Jews rejected the offered salvation but the Gentiles accepted it. This story introduces that theme. While this reading anticipates the Feast of the Epiphany, where it properly belongs, it is also appropriate here, since the Wise Men were making a religious pilgrimage.

The Epiphany, January 6

A

Theme: All the earth will come and worship him.

Psalm 72 [at the Eucharist: vss.1-2, 10-17]

Some scholars have interpreted this psalm as referring to the Messiah. Its appropriateness on this feast lies in the fact that the psalmist foresaw that kings of other lands would bow down before him (vss. 10-11, 15).

Isaiah 60:1-6, 9

The prophet assures the Babylonian exiles that God will save and restore his people. This will be witnessed by the nations, who will therefore come and worship the Savior God. The passage puts into poetry the message of the story of the Wise Men.

Ephesians 3:1-12

The theme of this epistle is that all people find their unity in Christ. So the writer logically holds the conviction that "Gentiles are fellow heirs, members of the same body, and partakers of the promise in Christ Jesus through the gospel" (v.6).

Matthew 2:1-12

The story of the Wise Men sets forth the Epiphany message in picture pageantry: Christ is recognized by representatives of the nations who come to worship him.

First Sunday after Epiphany

A

Theme: The baptism of Jesus

Psalm 89:1-29 [at the Eucharist: vss.20-29]

This long psalm is a lament at the time of some great national disaster. The first of its three parts (vss. 1-18) is a hymn of praise to God. The opening section of part two (vss. 19-29) deals with the great promises made to King David. When we hear them on this day we identify them with Jesus at the time of his baptism.

Isaiah 42:1-9

On the day on which we celebrate Jesus' baptism this "servant poem" from Second Isaiah is most appropriate. Regardless of whom the poet had in mind, the Christian identifies the Lord's servant with Jesus. "He is my chosen, in whom my soul delights; I have put my spirit upon him" (v.1).

(Lead in: *"Thus says the Lord, 'Behold my servant. . . .'"*)

Acts 10:34-38

To Peter's amazement, God calls Gentiles, not just Jews, to be believers in the risen Lord. This passage is part of his address to Cornelius and his household after that realization dawns. "Gentiles shall come to thy light"

(Isa. 60:3) is a major Epiphany theme. Peter, in telling Cornelius' household about Jesus, refers to the Lord's baptism: "anointed with the Holy Spirit and with power."

Matthew 3:13-17
The Epiphany season is the time when we celebrate the fact that Jesus was revealed to all (*epiphani*) as mankind's Savior. The first of the series of events which make this evident is his baptism by John: he is God's beloved and trusted Son. The words from heaven sound almost like an echo of the Isaiah poem above (Isa. 42:1).

Second Sunday after the Epiphany

A

Theme: The disciple must proclaim news of his Lord.

Psalm 40:1-10
In the opening verses of this psalm, the poet expresses deep gratitude for deliverance. However, given the discipleship theme of today's Scripture, such verses as, "Oh, that I could make your plans known and tell them!" and "I love to do your will, O my God," stand out prominently.

Isaiah 49:1-7
This day's Scripture contributes to our understanding of the meaning of discipleship. This "servant poem" states that discipleship involves demanding responsibilities. "It is too light a thing that you should be my servant. . . I will give you as a light to the nations. . ." (v.6).

I Corinthians 1:1-9
Being a Christian means that "you are called by God into the fellowship of his Son" (v.9), and because the God who calls us is faithful and can be depended upon to keep his promises, those who are members of that believing fellowship are saved by God's faithfulness. This is the wonder of belonging to Christ.

John 1:29-41
The Fourth Gospel contains much symbolism. When Jesus first appears, John the Baptist says, "Behold, the Lamb of God who takes away the sin of the world!" (v.29). This is what the writer is saying to the reader of his whole Gospel. The same is true of Peter's words to Andrew: "We have found the Messiah" (v.41).
(Lead in: *"The next day John saw Jesus. . . ."*)

Third Sunday after the Epiphany

A

Theme: The people of God.

Psalm 139:1-17 *[at the Eucharist: vss. 1-11]*

Here in an extraordinary hymn-prayer the psalmist is wrestling with the nature of God. He is all-knowing (vss. 1-5); he is omnipresent (vss. 6-11); he is the Creator (vss. 12-15). The psalmist concludes that man is unable to comprehend God's greatness. There is no question but that he belongs to God in a very intimate and special way.

Amos 3:1-8

The Church (*ecclesia*) is literally the "called-out" people. This designation was true of Israel, as Amos makes clear, and is the presupposition behind the writings of the N.T. (I Peter 2:9-10). As part of this people, the prophet Amos knows himself to be God's spokesman, as he here explains.

I Corinthians 1:10-17

The oneness of God's people is, in every age, threatened by the bickering littleness of individuals. This was in part the reason why Paul wrote this epistle. Our oneness is in Christ, not men. Later he elaborates on this theme by explaining that the Church is one body, not many (chap. 12), and by giving content to the meaning of love (chap. 13).

Matthew 4:12-23

After the arrest of John the Baptist (Mt. 14:3-4) Jesus begins his public ministry. Almost immediately he began to gather about him a group of disciples, intimate and constant followers, who became after the crucifixion-resurrection the nucleus of the new body of called-out people, the Christian Church.

(Lead in: *"Now when Jesus heard that John. . . ."*)

Fourth Sunday after the Epiphany

A

Theme: Seek to do God's will.

Psalm 37:1-23 *[at the Eucharist: vss. 1-6]*

This is more a collection of proverbs than a psalm. It is an old person's (v.25) advice to the young. In a fatherly way he vindicates the practice of religion.

Micah 6:1-8

In this dramatic passage, God speaks out in contention against Israel.

This is followed by Israel's questioning reply as to how God can best be served. Then the prophet tersely describes the behavior which pleases God. It may be that this interchange was in Paul's mind as he wrote his well-known description of Christian love (I Cor. 13:1-3).

I Corinthians 1: [18-25] 26-31
Paul argues that "the word of the cross" is not a new wisdom one can master and brag about. Rather, it is a call to belong to Christ, who becomes "the source of your life" (v.30). Worldly standards as to what is wise and what is foolish are now set aside.

Matthew 5:1-12
Our Lord's Beatitudes, describing those who are "blessed," put the capstone on the other readings heard on this day. Jesus pictures those who are blessed members of God's kingdom, another way of saying those who seek to do his will.

Fifth Sunday after the Epiphany

A

Theme: The salt of the earth and the light of the world.

Psalm 27 [at the Eucharist: vss. 1-7]
Here are two psalms which have been put together. (The same is true of Psalm 19.) The first (vss.1-8) expresses an unshakable trust in God. The second (vss.9-17) is the lament of one who is in need of help in his great distress.

Habakkuk 3:1-6, 17-19
The first two chapters of this little book deal with the problem of suffering. The author (or the editor?) thought it appropriate to close with a hymn of praise which expresses thanksgiving and trust in a time of want. Habakkuk stresses unwavering faith in God's merciful goodness in spite of distress—not the kind of faith for fair-weather believers.

I Corinthians 2:1-11
The apostle is seeking to make clear that the wisdom of God differs vastly from the wisdom of men. The former supplies the basis for a relationship with the crucified Christ through the Spirit; it is by that Spirit that one comes to know God. This is a very different thing from the wisdom of this age—a body of knowledge about temporal matters.

Matthew 5:13-20
These are memorable words from the Sermon on the Mount. The righteousness which grows out of a relationship with the crucified and risen

Lord exceeds that of the legalistic Pharisees. It transforms those who live by it so that they truly are the salt of the earth and the light of the world.

(Lead in: *"Jesus said, 'You are the salt. . . . ' "*)

Sixth Sunday after the Epiphany

A

Theme: The Christian's view of God's commandments

Psalm 119:1-16 [at the Eucharist: vss. 9-16]
This psalm is a long poem in praise of God's law. Those who walk in the law of the Lord are blameless in God's sight (v.1). This was a fundamental belief of the Pharisees, to which Jesus added deeper meaning. The second stanza here expresses fatherly concern for youth.

Ecclesiasticus 15:11-20
A wise and worldly man advises his son to live prudently.

I Corinthians 3:1-9
The apostle is seeking to deal with bickering and strife within the Corinthian congregation. The mature realization to which members of the church are to aspire is that all are God's fellow workers.

Matthew 5:21-24, 27-30, 33-37
In this part of the Sermon on the Mount, Jesus contrasts the righteousness of citizens of the kingdom of God with the moralism of the Pharisees, using commandments six, seven, and nine as examples. This contrasts sharply with the merely prudent behavior counselled in the Bible's Wisdom writings such as Ecclesiasticus.

(Lead in: *"Jesus said, 'You have heard. . . . ' "*)

Seventh Sunday after the Epiphany

A

Theme: Love your neighbor.

Psalm 71 [at the Eucharist: vss. 16-24]
Here is the prayer and lamentation of an older person of deep faith who is apparently in danger of persecution by malicious enemies. God is to him the "Holy One of Israel" (v.22), whose righteousness "reaches to the heavens" (v.19). His view is of a piece with that of the author of Leviticus. But the latter takes this holiness a step further, into neighbor relations (Lev. 19:18).

Leviticus 19:1-2, 9-18

Here is the ancient law from which our Lord's second great commandment comes (Mk. 12:28-31). God is holy and is to be revered. All God's creation is therefore holy and should be treated with reverence. This is the underlying reason for loving one's neighbor. Romans 12:19-21 might be considered an elaboration of vss. 17-18.

I Corinthians 3:10-11, 16-23

The O.T. law commands that each of us love his neighbor as himself. The apostle builds meaning into the self we are to love as a criterion for neighbor relations. One's self belongs to God and is to be held in reverence.

Matthew 5:38-48

In the Sermon on the Mount Jesus enlarges the meaning of the neighbor we are commanded to love to include our enemies as well as our friends. Our goal, he admonishes, is to strive to keep up with our heavenly Father in this matter.

(Lead in: *"Jesus said, 'You have heard. . . .' "*)

Eighth Sunday after the Epiphany   A

Theme: Trust in God.

Psalm 62 [at the Eucharist: vss. 6-14]

The psalmist is in a difficult situation; he is forsaken and even persecuted by former friends. His complete trust is put in God as his only stronghold.

Isaiah 49:8-18

In beautiful poetry the prophet sings of the day when the Lord will come and redeem the people of Israel. He is addressing the Jews in Babylonian exile. We hear his words as referring to our Lord and ourselves: no matter how difficult our lot, the Lord does not forsake us.

1 Corinthians 4:1-5, [6-7], 8-13

The apostle enlarges on what it means to be God's servant. Part of what he says is autobiographical and holds up standards of dedication which challenge us to be more faithful.

Matthew 6:24-34

In the Sermon on the Mount, Jesus issues this warning to those who would be his followers: to become anxious and put our trust in material things seduces us into transferring our allegiance from God to mammon (the things of this world).

(Lead in: *"Jesus said, 'no man can. . . .' "*)

Last Sunday after the Epiphany

A

Theme: The transfiguration of Christ.

Psalm 99

This is a hymn to God the Holy One (vss. 3, 5, 9). Because his worship is identified with "his holy hill," the settings for the giving of the Ten Commandments and the transfiguration come to mind.

Exodus 24:12 [13-14] 15-18

In the Bible, a cloud-topped mountain is a place of holiness. This is the setting in which Moses received the Ten Commandments. Both here and in the transfiguration of Jesus it is the setting in which God's presence is known.

Philippians 3:7-14

Because of the transfiguration and events surrounding it, Peter began to understand the meaning of the Lord's death and resurrection. Here Paul (in looking back on his own life) tells how he has grown into a comprehension of the inner meaning of the Lord's suffering, death, and resurrection.

Matthew 17:1-9

The transfiguration of Christ was a watershed of insight for his disciples. It marks the occasion of their realization that their Lord had fulfilled their ancient tradition, represented by Moses and Elijah. Beyond this point Jesus' coming passion becomes increasingly the focus of attention.

First Sunday in Lent

A

Theme: Man's sin and man's Savior

Psalm 51 [at the Eucharist: vss. 1-13]

This most important of the penitential psalms "demonstrates the essence of true penitence" (Weiser). The writer looks at his own spiritual condition with unabashed frankness. To the Christian, the words "Give me. . .your saving help. . .your bountiful Spirit" (v. 13) cannot but be associated with the Spirit of the risen Lord.

Genesis 2:4b-9, 15-17, 25-3:7
This is an edited version of the second creation story plus the account of the origin of humanity's sinfulness, known as the Fall of Man. This latter describes the way sin begins in each of us. "You will be like God" (v.5) was the fatal temptation. Sin is man's effort to become God's rival rather than being God's faithful child. Salvation history begins here: man's need for a savior begins with his fall.

Romans 5:12-19 [20-21]
Paul discusses the coming of sin into the world and what the coming of Jesus Christ means to sin-ridden humanity.

Matthew 4:1-11
Jesus was tempted to take matters into his own hands, as Adam and Eve did. Instead, he put deep meaning into the words, "Thy will, not mine, be done." Here we see him tempted as we are yet without sin (Heb. 4:15). He understands our need for help in temptation.

Second Sunday in Lent
A
Theme: The people of God

Psalm 33: 12-22
This portion of the psalm is a thanksgiving to God on behalf of the nation which looks back to Abraham as its patriarch. These people are they whom "he has chosen to be his own" (v.12). They are "those who wait upon his love" (v.18) and who put their trust in him (v.22).

Genesis 12:1-8
This tells of one of the significant decisions which has changed the course of human history. Abram obeyed the divine prompting, moved to a strange land, and became patriarch of the Hebrew people. The Bible's whole story, and the influence of Christianity on subsequent history, are the result.

Romans 4:1-5 [6-12] 13-17
In Paul's elaborate argument, he builds upon the religious insight of

Abraham. Abraham lived by faith; he is an example to believers in the risen Lord.

John 3:1-17

Like Abraham of old, Nicodemus, in his encounter with Jesus, was called upon to make a significant decision regarding his own salvation history.

Third Sunday in Lent

A

Theme: The water of life

Psalm 95 [at the Eucharist: vss. 6-11]

The first part of this psalm is familiar as the *Venite* (vss. 1-7a), in which the congregation is prepared for the impending encounter with God in worship. The latter part (vss. 7b-11) is a warning from God, including mention of Israel's grumblings for lack of water in the wilderness (v.8). The point is that it is not the rock from which Moses extracted water (for the places mentioned in v.8 see Exod. 17:7) but God himself who is "the rock of our salvation" (v.1).

Exodus 17:1-7

This is the second of three accounts of the Israelites complaining over lack of water in the wilderness (cf. Exod. 15:22-27; Num. 20:1-13). Moses had faith in God's presence and power and concern. It was this faith that made it possible for him to lead his people out of Egypt and made this a major chapter in the salvation history of God's chosen people.

Romans 5:1-11

Like Moses, the Christian is in the right with God (justified) because of his faith. But for the Christian this is faith in the crucified and risen Lord who has brought about our reconciliation.

John 4:5-26 [27-38] 39-42

In his conversation with the woman at the well, Jesus turns from the need for well water to "a spring of water welling up to eternal life" (v.14). He moves from her physical need to her spiritual need, and the encounter becomes a milestone in her salvation history.

(Lead in: *"So Jesus came to a city. . . ."*)

Fourth Sunday in Lent

A

Theme: Jesus, the light of the world

Psalm 23
The familiar shepherd psalm is identified with David but it also is stretched in our minds to include the Good Shepherd. Under this all-embracing concern, we shall lack nothing herein or hereafter. The Good Shepherd who leads us lights our way.

1 Samuel 16:1-13
The kingdom of Israel reached its greatest size, power, and influence during the reign of David. This greatness was projected into the future by thinking of the coming Messiah as the "son of David" (Mk. 12:35). The anointing of David as the future king heralds the beginning of Israel's greatness. So the occasion is a milestone in the salvation history of Israel.

Ephesians 5:[1-7] 8-14
In the ethical section of this epistle, the believer's attention is focused on Christ, who will throw light on the path of those who would be "imitators of God" (vss.1 and 14).

John 9:1-13 [14-27] 28-38
The account of Jesus healing the blind man makes light and salvation almost identical terms. "I am the light of the world," said Jesus (v.5). "Once you were darkness, but now you care light in the Lord," observed the writer of the Epistle (Eph. 5:8). Because a greater person than David has come, salvation is at hand.

Fifth Sunday in Lent

A

Theme: The Lord is the giver of life.

Psalm 130
The psalmist speaks from depths of despair brought on by sin, and then is able to rise to levels of assurance of divine forgiveness and grace. He experiences in his soul the death-to-life experience of Lazarus.

Ezekiel 37:1-3 [4-10] 11-14

To the faithful remnant in Babylonian captivity their nation seemed to be dead, a lost cause. They and their God had been defeated. The prophet's vision and his message of hope to them was that God could and would breathe new life into the nation of Israel and it would live again.

Romans 6:16-23

The Christian Church was the resurrection community in a sense that no O.T. prophet could have foreseen. Sin brings death, wrote the apostle, but "the free gift of God is eternal life through Christ Jesus" (v.23). To the believers in the risen Lord, Paul's words described a present reality.

John 11:[1-17] 18-44

Jesus' raising of Lazarus from the dead and the subsequent discourse give dramatic emphasis to Paul's words. "The free gift of God is eternal life through Christ Jesus" (Rom. 6:23).

Palm Sunday

A

Theme: The passion of Jesus Christ

Psalm 22:1-21 [at the Eucharist: vss. 1-11]

The prayer of a lonely, put-upon individual opens with those familiar words quoted by Jesus during his desolate hours on the cross. The similarity between the sufferings of Jesus and those of the psalmist is striking.

Isaiah 45:21-25

These several stanzas are from a poem (vss. 14-25) concerning the conversion of the nations. In them, God makes clear that he will triumph as the righteous God and Savior of "all the ends of the earth."

Alternate reading: Isaiah 52:13-53:12

This last of the four "servant of the Lord" poems scattered through Isaiah from chapters 42 to 53 describes one who humbly accepts suffering on behalf of his people. Scholars do not agree as to whether the servant is an individual, a dedicated remnant of the people, or the nation of Israel as a whole. In any case, we think of this passage as one of the spiritual high points of the O.T. and see in it a description of the meaning of Christ's passion.

Philippians 2:5-11

Here in a nutshell is Paul's belief about Jesus Christ. He who humbled himself to become a man and to die on the cross is the Lord of all.

Matthew [26:36-75] 27:1-54 [55-66]

This is the account of the passion and death of Jesus Christ. In its entirety it begins in the garden of Gethsemane, where he was arrested and includes his arraignment before the Sanhedrin, his trial by Pilate, crucifixion, death, and burial. The shorter version comprises the trial by the Roman governor, crucifixion, and death.

Easter Day

A

Theme: The resurrection of Christ

Psalm 118:14-29 [at the Eucharist: vss. 14-17, 22-24]

This psalm is "a powerful testimony to the strength of faith that flows from the direct experience of the help of God" (Weiser). After the introduction, there is the thanksgiving of an individual (vss. 5-21). The portion of this section which we read sounds like the thanksgiving of the risen Lord himself (vss. 18, 22). The latter part of the psalm (vss. 22-29) is the chorus of pilgrims attending the feast. Read on this day, it is an appropriate Easter hymn.

Acts 10:34-43

Peter was the leader of the Twelve and the first to see the risen Lord (Lk. 24:34). Here is part of one of this early sermons, in which it is obvious that the resurrection of Christ is of crucial importance.

Alternate first reading: Exodus 14:10-14, 21-25; 15:20-21

The Bible from beginning to end is saying that the meaning of creation is seen in the light of redemption. In a sense, the exodus from Egypt and the Lord's resurrection are the foci of salvation history. In the exodus we see the birth and establishment of the community of the old covenant. The resurrection stands in the same relation to the Christian Church.

Colossians: 3:1-4

The conviction that the risen Lord has conquered both sin and death is meant to influence all that the Christian is and does.

John 20: 1-10 [11-18]

The Easter morning account in John is, first of all, Mary Magdalene's story. She is baffled by the empty tomb, suspecting foul play, and she is the first to see the risen Lord. Her meeting him in the garden is peculiar to John and is one of the warmest and most touching of all the resurrection appearances. Included is the enigmatic command, "Do not touch me," and a perplexing reference to his impending ascension. There is no further allusion to the ascension in John, as there is in Luke.

Alternate Gospel: Matthew 28: 1-10

Each Gospel writer gives his own picture of Easter morning. Mark, the earliest account, tells of the empty tomb with astonishment, awe, and fear. Matthew in his turn adds details which transform the atmosphere into one of worship and joy. This forms a nice balance with the worship and joy with which the infant Jesus was first greeted (Mt. 2:10-11); the end is like the beginning.

Easter Evening

Theme: The risen Christ gives us new life in him.

Psalm 114

This is a hymn of praise to God because of the exodus, which is the fundamental saving act of the O.T. The Lord's resurrection is the fundamental saving act of God in the new covenant.

Alternate psalm: Psalm 136

This litany psalm bears witness to God's perpetual grace in creation and in history. A major event in that history is the exodus from Egypt (vss. 11-15), which is thought of as the O.T. counterpart of the resurrection.

Alternate psalm: Psalm 118:14-17, 22-24

This psalm is a powerful testimony to the strength of faith. The portion read here sounds like a hymn of thanksgiving for the Lord's resurrection.

Acts 5: 29a, 30-32

This is Peter's witness to the resurrection before the Sanhedrin.

Alternate first reading: Daniel 12:1-3

The Book of Daniel ends with visions of the last days. There will be a

time of general resurrection and judgment. This insight is reflected in the
N.T. (Jn. 5:29 and Acts 24:15). One of God's great gifts is suggested here:
the life that God has given each of us is precious, and he cares how we use it.

1 Corinthians 5:6b-8
Leaven has an infectious quality and was usually considered a symbol of
defilement. But it was also the sign of a new start, since its use meant that
there was no sour dough left from a previous baking. In the Passover ritual
unleavened bread was associated with the remembrance of Israel's
redemption from Egypt—a people's new start. Here Paul transfers that
ancient association to Christ's resurrection and the new start which is ours
because of the risen Christ.

Alternate Epistle: Acts 5:29a, 30-32 [see above]

Luke 24:13-35
Luke's Easter evening account is significant because the ways in which
those disciples knew the risen Lord are ways which are ours also: the
opening of the Scriptures and the breaking of bread—Word and
Sacrament.

(Lead in: *"That very day two of Jesus' followers were going. . . ."*)

Second Sunday of Easter   A

Theme: Christ's resurrection—fundamental Christian belief

Psalm 111
This festive hymn of praise is obviously appropriate for the Easter
season. The Christian naturally thinks of these words in terms of the fact
that God has raised Christ from the dead.

Alternate psalm: Psalm 118:19-24
On this day, these verses from the middle of a powerful hymn of faith are
associated with the Easter event. (See Easter Day above for a fuller analysis
of Psalm 118).

Acts 2:14a, 22-32
This is part of the first Christian sermon of which we have any record.
Peter delivered it on the streets of Jerusalem on the Jewish Feast of

Pentecost, which is fifty days after the Feast of the Passover at which Jesus was crucified. Notice that Peter is a brave, bold man in contrast to the fearful fellow who had denied Jesus at the time of his trial. Notice also that he is unshakably convinced that Jesus has risen from the dead.

Alternate to the Acts reading: Genesis 8:6-16; 9:8-16
This is the conclusion of the flood story. With the end of the flood, new life is begun, and the regular seasons and the rainbow are constant reminders of God's sustaining providence.

1 Peter 1:3-9
Peter is writing approximately two generations after the crucifixion-resurrection to Christians in a time of persecution; notice how central is his conviction of the Lord's resurrection.

Alternate Epistle: Acts 2: 14a, 22-32 [see above]

John 20:19-31
The earliest record of resurrection appearances is in 1 Corinthians 15:3-8. These fall into two categories. The first group (to Cephas or Peter *et al*) has a church-founding significance. The second group (to James *et al*) has a mission-inaugurating significance. The two appearances described in John 20 are in the first category. Jesus binds the disciples together in their conviction of his risen presence. The Holy Spirit is bestowed, and the Church as a spiritual entity begins.

Third Sunday of Easter
A
Theme: Believe in the risen Lord; know him in the breaking of bread.

Psalm 116 [at the Eucharist: vss.10-17]
The psalmist is filled with thankfulness because God has delivered him from some danger which threatened his life. The latter part of the reading has for the Christian overtones which suggest the Eucharist: "the cup of salvation" (v.11), "the sacrifice of thanksgiving" (v.15).

Acts 2:14a, 36-47
Fifty days after Jesus' crucifixion-resurrection (the Feast of Pentecost), Peter boldly preached the first Christian sermon on a Jerusalem street corner. Here are his concluding words and the effect of his sermon on those who heard him.

Alternate to the Acts of reading: Isaiah 43: 1-12
Some of the deepest spiritual insights of the O.T. are found in Second
Isaiah (40-66), and they anticipate in faith God's mighty revelation of
himself in the life, death, and resurrection of Jesus Christ. This poem is an
example. God describes himself as "your Savior"; "I have redeemed you"
(vss. 1 and 3). To the recipients of his goodness he says, "You are my
witnesses" (v.10).

1 Peter 1:17-23
In Acts 2 Peter is telling Jerusalem what the Lord's resurrection means
to him weeks after the event. Here, more than a generation later, he gives a
more profound view of what Christ's resurrection means.

Alternate Epistle: Acts 2: 14a, 36-47 [see above]

Luke 24:13-35
This resurrection appearance indicates something of the impetus which
caused the Lord's Supper to be so universally observed from the very first.
Jesus had evidently performed the mealtime ritual—"he took the bread and
blessed and broke it and gave it to them" (v. 30)—so many times with his
followers that the act was indelibly associated with remembrance of him.

Fourth Sunday of Easter

A

Theme: The Good Shepherd

Psalm 23
This is the familiar and beloved shepherd psalm.

Acts 6:1-9; 7:2a, 51-60
Organization began to develop early in the Christian Church. First there
were only the twelve apostles. Now seven assistants (Greek *diakonia*-dea-
cons) were selected to help them. The most outstanding of that group,
Stephen, became the first Christian martyr.

Alternate to the Acts reading: Nehemiah 9:6-15
Israel's faith throughout the O.T. is rehearsed as salvation
history—what God had done in choosing, delivering, and guiding his
people. Ezra's prayer on their behalf is obviously grounded in history. The
God of their fathers is truly "the Shepherd of Israel" (cf., Ps. 80).

1 Peter 2:19-25

Peter is writing to his fellow Christians in a time of persecution. The risen Christ who suffered for us has a shepherd's concern for those who "follow in his steps."

Alternate Epistle: Acts 6:1-9; 7:2a, 51-60 [see above]

John 10:1-10

Christian thinking of Christ as the Good Shepherd stems from this passage. In a time when shepherds keeping their flocks on rural hillsides were as common as our roadside service stations, to think of our Lord as the Good Shepherd was a powerful metaphor full of deep meaning.

(Lead in: *"Jesus said, 'Truly, truly. . . .' "*)

Fifth Sunday of Easter

A

Theme: The mighty Lord has done great things for us.

Psalm 66:1-11 [at the Eucharist: vss. 1-8]

Here is a hymn extolling the majesty of God as seen in his everlasting rule and his mighty saving works. To the Christian, his most awesome deed is the resurrection, by which he vanquished both sin and death.

Acts 17: 1-15

This is a brief picture of Paul's evangelistic travels through Macedonia and Greece. His message was that the risen Lord was the Christ (Messiah). Opposition to him came from orthodox Jews who created such an uproar in the towns he visited that the civil authorities were persuaded that Paul and his associates were "turning the world upside down."

(Lead in: *"Now when Paul and Silas had passed. . . ."*)

Alternate to the Acts reading: Deuteronomy 6:20-25

The Ten Commandments are in the previous chapter, and our Lord's "first and great commandment" is at the beginning of this chapter. Children of the Israelites learned of their religious heritage as a result of their questions growing out of observing their parents' piety, which was actually the behavior of gratitude (Deut. 4:33-40). There is wisdom here both as to why the law was observed and how children obtain religious education.

(Lead in: *"Moses said, 'When your son asks. . . .' "*)

1 Peter 2:1-10

   This extraordinary passage was written to Christians at a time when they were being persecuted. "You have tasted the kindness of the Lord," writes Peter. Because they believed their Lord had triumphed over all evil and had bestowed his victorious Spirit on his followers, they had a new identity.

Alternate Epistle: Acts 17:1-15 [see above]

John 14:1-14

   This familiar passage from Jesus' upper room discourse applies the significance of his resurrection to the lives of his believers.

   (Lead in *"Jesus said, Let not your hearts. . . .' "*)

Sixth Sunday of Easter (Rogation Sunday)

A

Theme: Nature proclaims divine truth.

Psalm 148 [at the Eucharist: vss. 7-14]

   Inanimate created things and living creatures unite in the praise of God their Creator and Preserver. Here on Rogation Sunday, all nature joins in the praise of God.

Acts 17:22-31

   While the N.T. contains a number of Paul's writings, this is one of the fullest accounts of his preaching. He knew how to take the situation at hand and turn it to his own ends.

Alternate to the Acts reading: Isaiah 41:17-20

   Here is a lovely, lyrical interlude in a long poem (41:1-42:4), in which an unknown poet sees in springs of water in a barren land evidence of God's concern for his people. It is especially appropriate because on the Rogation Days between now and Ascension Day (next Thursday) we will be asking God's blessing on our plantings.

1 Peter 3:8-18

   This epistle was addressed to Christians who lived in a time of persecution. They were enjoined to serve God faithfully and to avoid evil no matter what life's external circumstances. They were sustained by the assurance that, "If you do suffer for righteousness sake, you will be blessed. Have no fear. . . ." They believed this promise and the Church grew.

Alternate Epistle: Acts 17:22-31 [see above]

John 15:1-8
The vine and branches metaphor describing the relationship between Christ and his followers supplies us with much food for thought—and behavior. That which grows in the world of nature can help us understand the profound nature of God's relation to man.

(Lead in: *"Jesus said, 'I am the true vine. . . .' "*)

Seventh Sunday of Easter

A

Theme: The ascended Lord both reigns and prays for us

Psalm 68: 1-20
This is a complicated, involved psalm. It deals in part with the response of the praying community to the revelation of God. On this Sunday following the ascension it seems especially appropriate because of such expressions as these: "Magnify him who rides upon the heavens" (v.4) and "You have gone up on high" (v.18).

Alternate psalm: Psalm 47
A part of the thinking about Christ's ascension is that he is enthroned in heaven and recognized as Lord of all. This is a major theme in Ascensiontide hymns. Therefore, depicting the enthronement of God as this psalm does, is quite appropriate. "God has gone up with a shout." He "sits upon his holy throne" and is "King of all the earth" (vss. 5, 6, 8).

Acts 1: [1-7] 8-14
At the beginning of Luke's second volume (see Lk. 1:1-4) we have the commissioning of the disciples to carry on the work their Lord has begun (vss. 1 and 8). Then comes the last of the resurrection appearances—the risen Christ ascends into heaven. This is in no sense a final separation. The promise of the Spirit—*his* Spirit and presence—makes this an occasion of great joy (Lk. 24:52-53).

Alternate to the Acts reading: Ezekiel 39:21-29
This is the conclusion of a series of oracles and it deals with the restoration of Israel after the Babylonian captivity. In this oracle of God to the prophet the captivity and restoration are seen as mighty divine acts that "all the nations shall see" (v.21).

1 Peter 4:12-19
The second generation after the crucifixion-resurrection was a time of persecution for faithful Christians. Peter assures his readers that the Spirit of the risen Christ will abide with them in the midst of their "fiery ordeal."

Alternate Epistle: Acts 1:[1-7] 8-14 [see above]

John 17:1-11
This is Christ's high priestly prayer for the unity of the Church. It gives us an intimate glimpse into his thinking about his relation to the Father, his vocation and ministry, and his deep concern for the company of all faithful people.

Day of Pentecost

A

Theme: The Spirit of the Lord

Psalm 104:25-37 [at the Eucharist: vss. 25, 28-31]
This psalm is one of the most beautiful poems in the Psalter. Here is in effect the creation story of Genesis set to music. The Pentecost overtones of this psalm are in v. 31: "You send forth your breath (Spirit), and they are created; and so you renew the face of the earth."

Alternate psalm: Psalm 33 [at the Eucharist: vss. 12-15, 18-22]
This psalm was probably composed "for the Covenant Festival which was celebrated at New Year" (Weiser). Pentecost is in a sense that Covenant Festival for the Christian. The people with a special relationship to God (v.12) are those who are of the company in which the Holy Spirit dwells.

Acts 2:1-11
The first Christian Pentecost occurred on the ancient Jewish feast of that name, fifty days after that Feast of the Passover during which the crucifixion of Jesus had taken place. This day was the occasion on which the believers in the risen Lord first became aware of God's Spirit in their midst. Pentecost marks the beginning of the dynamic missionary life of the Christian Church.

Alternate reading: Ezekiel 11:17-20
Ezekiel's promise of restoration to exiled Israel sounds similar to the Pentecost event—a body of believers bound together by the Spirit of God.

(Lead in: omit *"Therefore say"*, begin, *"Thus says the Lord God. . . ."*)

1 Corinthians 12:4-13
The gifts of the Spirit are various, and Paul seeks to make this clear, at the same time stressing that those varied gifts all come from the same Spirit.

Alternate Epistle: Acts 2:1-11 [*see above*]

John 20:19-23
Here the risen Lord bestows his Holy Spirit on his disciples. In the Luke-Acts tradition, this is a separate occasion from the resurrection (Acts 2:1-11).

(Lead in: *"On the evening of Easter day. . . ."*)

Alternate reading: John 14:8-17
This part of Jesus' upper room discourse is appropriate on this feast because it throws light on the nature and function of the Holy Spirit.

First Sunday after Pentecost: Trinity Sunday

A

Theme: One God: the Creator, Jesus, and his Spirit

Psalm 150
While God has revealed himself to us as Father, Son, and Holy Spirit, he is still unquestionably one God. With the psalmist, we can exult in our worship and praise of him.

In place of the Psalm: Benedictus es, Domine (Canticle 2 or 13)
This is a hymn in praise of the God of Abraham, Isaac, and Jacob.

Genesis 1:1-2:3
This first of the two creation stories in Genesis gives a classic picture of God the Creator.

II Corinthians 13: [5-10] 11-14
"The God of love and peace" (v.11) is with us in a very special

way "Jesus Christ is in you"(v.5). The Spirit of the risen Christ motivates the lives of his worshipping, believing followers.

Matthew 28:16-20

These words, known as the Great Commission, express the driving compulsion of the Church from the earliest times. The creation story tells of mankind's first birth; here is the rebirth brought about by the coming of Jesus Christ.

The Season after Pentecost
Directions for the use of the Propers which follow are on page vi of the Introduction.
Proper 1   (Closest to May 11)

A

Theme: The Christian's view of God's commandments

Psalm 119:1-16 [at the Eucharist: vss. 9-16]

This psalm is a long poem in praise of God's law. Those who walk in the law of the Lord are blameless in God's sight (v.1) This was a fundamental belief of the Pharisees, to which Jesus added deeper meaning. The second stanza here expresses fatherly concern for youth.

Ecclesiasticus 15:11-20

A wise and worldly man advises his son to live prudently.

I Corinthians 3:1-9

The apostle is seeking to deal with the bickering and strife within the Corinthian congregation. The mature realization to which members of the church are to aspire is that all are God's fellow workers.

Matthew 5:21-24, 27-30, 33-37

In this part of the Sermon on the Mount, Jesus contrasts the righteousness of citizens of the kingdom of God with the moralism of the Pharisees, using commandments six, seven, and nine as examples. This contrasts sharply with the merely prudent behavior counselled in wisdom writings such as Ecclesiasticus.

(Lead in: *"Jesus said, 'You have heard. . . .' "*)

Proper 2 (Closest to May 18)

A

Theme: Love your neighbor

Psalm 71 [at the Eucharist: vss. 16-24]
Here is the prayer and lamentation of an older person of deep faith who is apparently in danger of persecution by malicious enemies. God is to him the "Holy One of Israel" (v.22) whose righteousness "reaches to the heavens" (v.19). His view is similar to that of the author of Leviticus. But the latter takes this holiness a step further, into neighbor relations (Lev. 19:18).

Leviticus 19:1-2, 9-18
Here is the ancient law from which our Lord's second great commandment comes (Mk. 12:28-31). God is holy and is to be revered. All God's creation is therefore holy and should be treated with reverence. This is the underlying reason for loving one's neighbor. Romans 12:19-21 might be considered an elaboration of vss. 17-18.

I Corinthians 3:10-11, 16-23
The O.T. law commands that each of us love his neighbor as himself. The apostle builds meaning into the self we are to love as a criterion for neighbor relations. One's self belongs to God and is to be held in reverence.

Matthew 5:38-48
In the Sermon on the Mount Jesus enlarges the meaning of the neighbor we are commanded to love to include our enemies as well as our friends. Our goal, he admonishes, is to strive to keep up with our heavenly Father in this matter.

Proper 3 (Closest to May 25)

A

Theme: Trust in God.

Psalm 62 [at the Eucharist: vss. 6-14]
The psalmist is in a difficult situation; he is forsaken and even persecuted by former friends. His complete trust is put in God as his only stronghold.

Isaiah 49:8-18
In beautiful poetry the prophet sings of the day when the Lord will come

and redeem the people of Israel. He is addressing the Jews in Babylonian exile. We hear his words as referring to our Lord and ourselves; no matter how difficult our lot, the Lord does not forsake us.

I Corinthians 4:1-5, [6-7], 8-13
The apostle enlarges on what it means to be God's servant. Part of what he says is autobiographical and holds up standards of dedication which challenge us to be more faithful.

Matthew 6:24-34
In the Sermon on the Mount, Jesus issues this warning to those who would be his followers: to become anxious and put our trust in material things seduces us into transferring our allegiance from God to mammon (the things of this world).
(Lead in: *"Jesus said, 'No man can. . . .' "*)

Proper 4 (Closest to June 1)

A

Theme: The importance of faith and works

Psalm 31 [at the Eucharist: vss. 1-5, 19-24]
This is the prayer of lamentation and thanksgiving of one who has suffered from illness (v.10), persecution (v.4), and being shunned by friends (v.11). He finds in God his refuge and strength (vss. 19-22) and counsels others that the way of faith is the source of one's strength in adversity (vss. 23-24).

Deuteronomy 11:18-21, 26-28
Moses enjoins the Israelites to keep God's commands as a way of life for themselves and the way they are to teach their children. The most effective parental teaching is example, as he has made clear earlier (Deut. 6:20-25).
(Lead in: *"Moses said, 'You shall lay up these words of mine. . . .' "*)

Romans 3:21-25a, 28
The apostle puts keeping God's commandments in Christian perspective. The Christian strives to do those things which are good and acceptable to God. But were this the whole of the matter, it would lead the insensitive to arrogance and snobbery, and the sensitive to guilt and remorse. Paul calls such a dilemma "this body of death" (Rom. 7:24). The good news is that we are justified in God's sight by our faith in his merciful goodness, not by our works of the law.

Matthew 7:21-27
In the Sermon on the Mount Jesus explains that our behavior is an

indication of our sincerity. Striving to do the Lord's will gives the ring of authenticity to our profession of faith.

(Lead in: *"Jesus said, 'Not every one. . . .' "*

Proper 5 (Closest to June 8)

A

Theme: Beware lest one's holiness dishonors God.

Psalm 50 [at the Eucharist: vss. 7-15]

The setting of this dramatic psalm is before the throne of the eternal Judge (vss. 1-6). He denounces those who dishonor him through the sacrificial cult (vss. 7-15), and denounces the immoral ways of the wicked (vss. 16-21). The conclusion contains warning and threat, exhortation and promise. (Note: the central section is of a piece with the Hosea passage quoted by Jesus, but it is hoped that the whole psalm will be used.)

Hosea 5:15-6:6

This oracle contains the musings of God (5:15), then the insincere, even cynical, musings of unfaithful Israel (6:1-3), and finally God's pronouncement of judgment against his unfaithful people (6:4-6). These words make clear Luther's comment that God's wrath is the underside of his love. (For clarity's sake certainly the word "saying" (5:15) should be omitted. Perhaps inserting the words, *"But Israel thinks in his heart. . . .,"* will help to convey the intended meaning.)

Romans 4:13-18

This is part of Paul's longer explanation (3:31-4:25) of justification by faith as fulfillment of the covenant with Abraham.

Matthew 9:9-13

Jesus' detailed knowledge of Scripture is amazing. Here in the face of the bigoted narrowness of the Pharisees he quotes the Hosea oracle (Hos. 6:6).

Proper 6 (Closest to June 15)

A

Theme: Reconciled to God and commissioned by him

Psalm 100

The familiar words of the *Jubilate Deo* sum up in poetry our response to the good news proclaimed in this day's Scripture. Let all lands be joyful and serve the Lord, for his mercy is everlasting and his faithfulness can always be depended upon.

Exodus 19:2-8a

The significance of this passage is that God's covenant is with the nation, not just her leaders. Moreover, as the priests and Levites had access to the altar and rejoiced in the service of God and the support of the faithful, so now the nation would fill the role of priest in the world—"a kingdom of priests and a holy nation" (v.6). Israel was to be "the Church," just as the New Israel was to have that role centuries later.

(Lead in: *"When the people of Israel set out. . . ."*)

Romans 5:6-11

Here is one of the most profoundly comforting passages in the New Testament. In spite of our sins, we are reconciled to God by the death of Jesus; we are "saved by his life" (resurrection). This is the ground of our faith and the source of our motivation.

Matthew 9:35-10:8 [9-15]

The laborers who are to tell people the good news that they are reconciled to God are few. Here, in the appointment of the twelve apostles, is the beginning of the New Israel charged and commissioned to proclaim and demonstrate that " the kingdom of God is at hand" (v.7).

Proper 7 (Closest to June 22)

A

Theme: The hard lot of the faithful witness

Psalm 69:1-18 [at the Eucharist:vss. 7-10, 16-18]

The psalm is the personal lament of one who is persecuted. After Psalm 22, Psalm 69 is the most frequently quoted in the New Testament in referring to Christ. In this context, we identify the psalmist's lament with Jeremiah in his dungeon and the sufferings Jesus tells his disciples they are about to undergo.

Jeremiah 20:7-13

Because of his honesty and courage in telling the leaders of Jerusalem the dire things God has revealed to him, Jeremiah was thrown into prison. His prayer is an impatient wrestling with God. It gives us a glimpse of the travail of soul of a tormented man of God.

Romans 5:15b-19

In this portion of the Sunday-by-Sunday course reading of Romans, Paul explains how the coming of Jesus Christ turned things aound and made new life possible for all of us.

(Lead in: *"For if many died through one man's trespass, i.e. Adam's,. . . "*)

Matthew 10: [16-23] 24-33

This is a part of Jesus' instruction to the Twelve before sending them out into the towns and villages of Judea to announce that "the kingdom of heaven is at hand" (v.7). He tells them that they will be persecuted, then comforts them: "Have no fear of them. . .every one who acknowledges me before men, I will also acknowledge before my Father who is in heaven" (vss. 26,32).

(Lead in: *"Jesus said, 'Behold, I send you. . . .' "*)

Proper 8 (Closest to June 29)

A

Theme: The coming of the Lord is a time of judgment.

Psalm 89:1-18 [at the Eucharist: vss. 1-4, 15-18]

On the coming day of the Lord, how shall one react? The psalmist says in this hymn of praise: Happy are the people who walk in the light of his presence (v. 15).

Isaiah 2:10-17

The opening five chapters of Isaiah are denunciations against those who have rebelled against God. The day of the Lord will be the time when the Lord alone is exalted in all his majesty, and the haughtiness of man, which separates him from both God and his fellows, will be brought low.

Romans 6:3-11

The profound meaning of Christian baptism is found here.

Matthew 10:34-42

In the concluding part of Jesus' instruction to his disciples before sending them forth to preach the kingdom of God, he makes it clear that the coming of the Lord will be a time of judgment rather than a time of easy bliss. His presence and his demands will attract some and repel others, setting even members of the same household against one another.

(Lead in: *"Jesus said, 'Do not think that. . . .' "*)

Proper 9 (Closest to July 6)

A

Theme: The kingdom, the power, and the glory

Psalm 145 [at the Eucharist: vss. 8-14]

This poem describes God's kingdom. Along with other O.T. passages (like Zech. 9:9f.) it gives us the background for a fuller appreciation of Jesus' prayer of thanksgiving heard on this day.

Zechariah 9:9-12

In an oracle concerning the triumph of the messianic king are these reassuring words, "Return to your stronghold, O prisoners of hope" (v.12).

Romans 7:21-8:6

In chapter 7 Paul has wrestled with the function of the law and sin. Here he deals with the final despair to which the law and sin bring one, and the release which comes through Christ Jesus.

Matthew 11:25-30

Matthew tells of Jesus instructing disciples whom he sends out in his name to preach the kingdom of God (10:5-11:1). He never actually tells of their return and report, as does Luke (Lk. 10:17-22). However, this passage suggests that they have returned, and its partial parallel to Luke substantiates that fact. Here is the messianic triumph which Zechariah foretold coupled with some of the most reassuring words in the Gospel.

Proper 10 (Closest to July 13)

A

Theme: The word of God goes forth.

Psalm 65 [at the Eucharist: vss. 9-14]

The psalmist sees in the blessing of much-needed rainfall (vs. 9-14) a wider context of thanksgiving: the rain is concrete evidence of the whole redemptive work of God. To experience God's providence at one point means to know him in all his fullness. God is addressed as the "hope of all the ends of the earth" (v.5).

Isaiah 55:1-5, 10-13

In glorious poetry the author of Second Isaiah writes of the word of God. "Hear that your soul may live" (v.3). In a later stanza he describes the activity and mission of the word of God. "The word goes forth. . . it shall not return to me empty" (v. 11).

Romans 8:9-17

The Sunday-by-Sunday serial reading of this epistle continues. Chapter 8 describes life in the Spirit. Paul uses "Spirit," "Spirit of God," and "Spirit of Christ." All of these refer to the Spirit of the risen Lord which he gave to his disciples after his resurrection (Jn. 20:22; Acts 1:2, 8; Gal.

5:22-24). The Spirit of the risen Christ is the motivating force in the life of the Christian believer.

Matthew 13:1-9, 18-23

Jesus' parable of the sower is about the word of God and the ways in which it is received. Both Jesus and Isaiah are dealing with the same theme. The Isaiah reading on this day gives us an appreciation of the word, its activity, its outreach, its power. Jesus' parable deals with the way it is received and challenges us.

Proper 11 (Closest to July 20)

A

Theme: The righteous will not fear in the judgment.

Psalm 86 [at the Eucharist: vss. 11-17]

This psalm is the earnest prayer of an individual who sincerely desires to live a life pleasing to God. "Teach me your way, O Lord, and I will walk in your truth" (v.11).

Wisdom 12:13, 16-19

This is part of a long argument the Jewish author addresses to Gentile readers. In form it is addressed to God, but it is not a prayer. He is stating that God is the source of righteousness; he is almighty and merciful.

Romans 8:18-25

In this portion of Pauls's eighth chapter description of life in the Spirit, he makes clear that our hope is in Christ. God will, in his own good time, redeem not only those who put their faith in the risen Lord but his whole creation.

Matthew 13:24-30, 36-43

Jesus' parable of the tares is a parable of judgment. While wheat and tares are growing together, the unbelieving conclude that God is weak and can be ignored. But the time of harvest comes. As the author of Wisdom put it, "Thou dost show thy strength when men doubt the completeness of thy power" (Wis. 12:17). Because of this, the righteous man is filled with good hope (Wis. 12:19).

Proper 12 (Closest to July 27)

A

Theme: Be open to God's truth.

Psalm 119:121-136 [at the Eucharist: vss. 129-136]

This long, artificially constructed psalm deals with keeping God's commandments. These two stanzas have some appropriateness on this day because they stress the need for understanding (vss. 125 and 130).

I Kings 3:5-12

Solomon succeeded David on the throne of Israel. The distinctive characteristic of the early years of his reign was his wise and discerning mind. This trait is related to a dream he had of an encounter with God shortly after ascending the throne.

Romans 8:26-34

This middle section of Paul's chapter on life in the Spirit makes it clear that the Spirit is our helper, in prayer as well as in works. He also makes it clear that nothing is out of the hands of God, and that the crucified and risen Christ is the agent of our salvation.

Matthew 13:31-33, 44-49a

Matthew has grouped together a number of Jesus' little parables about the kingdom of heaven. Over and over he makes the point that the wise, the discerning, the determined, and the dedicated are those who find their way into the kingdom. Solomon was wise and discerning in managing temporal affairs; Jesus urges us to be equally so in relation to eternal affairs.

(Lead in: *"Another parable Jesus put. . . ."*)

Proper 13 (Closest to August 3)

A

Theme: God's watchful providence

Psalm 78:1-29 [at the Eucharist: vss. 14-20, 23-25]

Israel's faith is historical, not philosophical. It grew out of reflection on the way God had dealt with the people's ancestors in former days. Other psalms recount this history (Pss. 105, 106), but in this one the poet reflects on "that which we have heard and known" (v.3).

Nehemiah 9:16-20

This whole chapter is a penitential psalm in the course of which Ezra the priest reviews God's concern for the Israelites in bringing them out of Egypt and during their trek through the wilderness.

(Lead in: *"Ezra said, 'O Lord God, our fathers acted. . . .' "*)

Romans 8:35-39

Here is the conclusion and climax of the chapter on the life of the Spirit. The O.T. priest could say, God cares about Israel and did not forsake her in the wilderness. Paul goes further: Nothing, no matter how dire, "will be able to separate us from the love of God in Christ Jesus our Lord" (v.39).

Matthew 14:13-21

The lesson of the great occasion when Jesus fed the five thousand is that he had compassion on the multitude, healed the sick, and fed them. This foretaste of the heavenly banquet is told six times in four Gospels. It made vivid Israel's ancient conviction that the gracious God abounds in steadfast love (cf., Neh. 9:17).

Proper 14 (Closest to August 10)

A

Theme: The Almighty who is Lord over nature cares for his people.

Psalm 29

This psalm is an interlude in the Jonah story while the prophet was in the belly of the fish. Actually, it is a hymn of thanksgiving after deliverance from "the waters." It sounds a bit premature because the psalm is probably a later addition to the story.

Jonah 2:1-9

This psalm is an interlude in the Jonah story while the prophet was in the belly of the fish. Actually, it is a hymn of thanksgiving after deliverance from the waters. It sounds a bit premature because the psalm is probably a later addition to the story.

Romans 9:1-5

Paul begins the part of his epistle dealing with the place of Jew and Gentile in God's purpose (chaps. 9-11) with this wholehearted appreciation of Israel.

Matthew 14:22-33

This miraculous episode takes place immediately after the feeding of the five thousand. Jesus had already revealed himself as Lord over the winds and the sea (8:23f.), so that is not the main point. The emphasis here is on the terror and fear of the disciples when separated from their Lord. Because he cares deeply about them he miraculously comes to them, and their physical fear turn to awe.

(Lead in: *"Then Jesus made the disciples. . . ."*)

Proper 15 (Closest to August 17)

A

Theme: Salvation is for all the peoples of the earth.

Psalm 67

This harvest festival hymn is appropriate today because v.2 is of a piece with the other readings. "Let your ways be known upon earth, your saving health among all nations."

Isaiah 56:1 [2-5] 6-7

In the latter part of what is known as Second Isaiah is a poem of prophetic admonitions and promises. This part of it shows the universality of God's concern for mankind.

Romans 11:13-15, 29-32

It was difficult for a Jew, one of God's chosen people, to realize that God desires to include all humanity in his plan of salvation. Paul, the apostle to the Gentiles, here gives his rationale for the place of Gentiles in the divine plan of salvation.

Matthew 15:21-28

Matthew's Gospel is pro-Jewish, but as it was written about two generations after the crucifixion-resurrection the author was aware of and reconciled to the Gentiles' place in the Christian Church, the new Israel. The writer's point of view is that the time before the crucifixion is the time when the Gospel was offered to Jews; after the resurrection is the time for preaching to the Gentiles. This accounts for his additions to this story, which he got from Mark (7:24-30).

Proper 16 (Closest to August 24)

A

Theme: Salvation is at hand.

Psalm 138

In the context of today's Scripture, this psalm of thanksgiving is heard as wholehearted thanksgiving because God has made good his purpose of salvation.

Isaiah 51:1-6

In a poem about the coming salvation (51:1-16) the prophet comforts the Babylonian exiles with the thought that God's "deliverance draws near speedily" (v.5). However, he sets the longed-for deliverance in a broader context: "My salvation will be for ever, and my deliverance will never be ended" (v.6).

Romans 11:33-36

Paul's discussion of the place of Jew and Gentile in the eternal purposes of God ends with this doxological outburst on God's inscrutable wisdom.

Matthew 16:13-20

Peter is the recognized leader of the Twelve in all of the Gospels, although Matthew accents this more than the others (e.g., adding "first" in 10:2). In this watershed event Peter puts into words the growing conviction of the Twelve as to who Jesus really is.

Proper 17 (Closest to August 31)

A

Theme: Rebuked by the Lord

Psalm 26 [at the Eucharist: vss. 1-8]

Here is a psalm of innocence that probably stems from a temple ceremony of late Judaism carried out by one who considered himself unjustly condemned of a capital offense. He fears that his end is imminent (v.9). This is the humble prayer of a godly person who is in imminent danger.

Jeremiah 15:15-21

Here is one of the bitterest outcries of the prophet's whole life. The Lord's reply shows that he needs to repent of his mood and be careful to speak only what is true. "Few passages in the Old Testament are as revealing as this one for the personality of Jeremiah and for the nature and function of the Hebrew prophet" (*Interpreter's Bible*).

Romans 12:1-8

This is the beginning of the ethical section of Paul's epistle. First he speaks of the duty of finding and doing God's will; then, in discussing love within the Church, he says that each individual must be subordinated to the whole body.

Matthew 16:21-27

Immediately after Peter has first called him "the Christ" (v.16), Jesus begins explaining to the disciples the kind of Christ (Messiah) he is: one who suffers and dies. Peter objects and Jesus rebukes him. Peter, and Jeremiah before him, were both dedicated to the Lord. Both spoke out in objection to God's ways; both were rebuked.

Proper 18 (Closest to September 7)

A

Theme: Repentance is the door into God's favor.

Psalm 119:33-48 [at the Eucharist: vss 33-40]
These two stanzas of this long psalm express the set of mind of one who seeks to hear and to heed God's word. "Behold, I long for your commandments. . . . let your loving mercy come to me, O Lord" (vss. 40, 41).

Ezekiel 33: [1-6] 7-11
This is the first in a series of oracles on responsibility. It is the prophet's responsibility to warn the people of Israel of impending doom if they do not repent. Even in this ominous passage it is clear that God is more interested in the repentence of the wicked person than in his death.

Romans 12:9-21
The ethical section of this epistle deals here with one's behavior toward others within the Church and his behavior toward enemies.

Matthew 18:15-20
The passage deals with the sheep that goes astray. Every effort is to be made to bring him to repentance: first in private, then before a few, finally before the whole assembly of disciples. In that full assembly the decision of the Church will be the decision of God. Matthew's Gospel, written some two generations after the crucifixion-resurrection, is really dealing here with community problems in the Church of his day.

Proper 19 (Closest to September 14)

A

Theme: Forgive that the Lord may be forgiving.

Psalm 103 [at the Eucharist: vss. 8-13]
This psalm has been called "one of the finest blossoms on the tree of Biblical faith" (Weiser). There is repeated reference to God's merciful forgiveness (vss. 3, 8, 10, 11), which makes it appropriate on this day.

Ecclesiasticus 27:30-28:7
The sage's advice regarding anger throws considerable light on the meaning of the Lord's Prayer petition, "Forgive us our trespasses, as we forgive those who trespass against us."

Romans 14:5-12
The closing part of Paul's epistle contains this wise advice about being sensitive to others' mode of life and way of expressing their dedication.

Matthew 18:21-35

Peter's question about forgiveness was the occasion for our Lord's parable of the unforgiving slave. What Ecclesiaticus put in a logical explanation, Jesus makes clear in a parable.

Proper 20 (Closest to September 21)

A

Theme: Angry with God

Psalm 145 [at the Eucharist: vss. 1-8]

The psalmist knows God to be "merciful in his deeds" and "loving in his works" (vss. 14, 18). His conviction is instructive to those who are angry with God.

Jonah 3: 10-4:11

This climax of the Jonah story is almost overlooked because of the more spectacular earlier part. Because the Ninevites believed Jonah's preaching and repented, God did not carry out the dire warning he had issued through the prophet. Jonah was angry because this undercut his rating as a prophet. He went out on a hillside and pouted. The author humorously pictures the merciful God and his sulking, spoiled-child prophet.

Philippians 1:21-27

Paul writes to the church at Philippi from prison (v.13). We catch a glimpse of both his inner feelings and his deep pastoral concern.

Matthew 20:1-16

Matthew thinks of the owner of the vineyard as God, and the reward eternal life. The parable really illustrates the owner's words, "I choose to give to this last as I give to you" (v.14). God is not answerable to man for what he does with his rewards. We get angry with God because we do not comprehend this.

Proper 21 (Closest to September 28)

A

Theme: Humbly repent and seek to do God's will.

Psalm 25:1-14 [at the Eucharist: vss. 3-9]

Here is the pensive prayer of a penitent who seeks forgiveness for his misdeeds and earnestly desires, as Paul put it, "to will and to do" God's good pleasure (see especially vss. 10 and 13). Because it was probably "composed in the quiet of a lonely life, it is. . . a perpetual source of comfort for people who are lonely or forsaken" (Weiser).

Ezekiel 18:1-4, 25-32
This whole chapter concerns each individual's responsibility to God for his behavior.

Philippians 2:1-13
In Paul's discussion of the Christian life he has inserted an eloquent and almost lyrical description of the essential meaning of the incarnation (vss. 5, 11). It has been called "the chief glory of the Epistle to the Philippians" (*The Interpreter's Bible*).

Matthew 21:28-32
This parable is related to the unbelief of the religious leaders of the Jews. As it is used here it contrasts "the response of the sinners to John, and the disobedience of the Jewish leaders to Jesus" (Fenton: *Matthew*). Originally, the parable probably was used by Jesus to illustrate the difference between saying and doing, which is a theme he deals with on several occasions (7:21; 12:50).
(Lead in: *"Jesus said, 'What do you think?. . . ' "*)

Proper 22 (Closest to October 5)

A

Theme: The vineyard of the Lord

Psalm 80 [at the Eucharist: vss. 7-14]
This is a lament about the dire fortunes of Israel, depicted here as an arbor of grape vines. There is a pleading refrain for restoration and salvation (cf. Num 6:24-26).

Isaiah 5:1-7
The song of the Lord's vineyard is an oracle of doom against Israel and Judah couched in a minstrel's song. God's people have failed their intended vocation as the chosen of the Lord.

Philippians 3:14-21
In the Sunday-by-Sunday serial reading of this epistle, we come to this glimpse at Paul's inner self. It both helps us understand him better and raises our standards of what it means to be Christ's faithful servant.

Matthew 21:33-43
The people of Israel were the vineyard of the Lord (Isa. 5:7). The

religious leaders in Jesus' parable are the vinedressers. The parable as it stands has become an allegory foretelling what those people in their self-interest would do to Jesus.

(Lead in: *"Jesus said, 'Hear another parable. . . .'"*)

Proper 23 (Closest to October 12)

A

Theme: The banquet of the Lord

Psalm 23

The shepherd psalm speaks picturesquely of the way the Lord watches over his people. A part of the blessing and joy of being under the Lord's protection is the pleasure of dining as guest of so loving a host.

Isaiah 25:1-9

The first part of this reading is a thanksgiving hymn for victory. The second is an eschatological musing that ultimately there will be a feast of triumph and the end of sorrow. These two are tied together by the thought that the Lord watches over Israel.

Philippians 4:4-13

These words are the apostle's closing admonitions. Here is dedication and a quietly joyful faith which is the ground of both his inner peace and of his treatment of others.

Matthew 22:1-14

Actually, here are two parables: the invitations to the wedding and the wedding garment. Together they represent the marriage feast as the life of the age to come; outside, "the outer darkness," is hell. The joys of that eschatological feast can be thought of as those of the banquet to which people who refused an invitation or who lacked repentance (a wedding garment—the proper attire of the soul) were not worthy to share.

Proper 24 (Closest to October 19)

A

Theme: God, the righteous Judge, is over all nations and peoples.

Psalm 96 [at the Eucharist: vss. 1-9]

The psalmist sings exultantly to the Lord who is the righteous Judge and will come to judge all peoples and nations.

Isaiah 45:1-7

The prophet's central conviction is that God is Lord over all. "There is none beside me" (v.6). God uses even the skill and might of Cyrus, the king of Persia, to carry out his purposes.

I Thessalonians 1:1-10

Paul's epistle begins with a thanksgiving for his brethren in the church at Thessalonica.

Matthew 22:15-22

This is one of the series of forensic encounters during Holy Week. The Pharisees try to trap Jesus into saying the Jews should not pay taxes to the Romans and thus get him in trouble with the authorities. It was popularly thought that coins belonged to him whose image they bore. Jesus is saying that just as we should give Caesar what belongs to him so also we should return to the Lord of all what belongs to him.

Proper 25 (Closest to October 26)

A

Theme: The summary of the law

Psalm 1

The psalmist probably had an educational motive when he composed this simple contrast between the good and the bad. On this day it stands out that the person is happy (blessed) who "delights in the law of the Lord" (v.2).

Exodus 22:21-27

In the course of a section of moral and religious laws are these verses of compassionate concern for one's neighbor. It is out of this sort of concern that the neighbor commandment quoted by our Lord comes (Lev. 19:18).

I Thessalonians 2:1-8

In reviewing his work among the people of Thessalonica the apostle also gives us a glimpse of the way he probably behaved in every place as he went about the work of spreading the Gospel of Jesus Christ.

Matthew 22:34-46

In the course of interrogating Jesus in an effort to trap him in some unwise, unpopular, or illegal statement, the question of the great commandment was put to him. This was a popular subject with the Pharisees. Jesus' reply is perhaps the first time the neighbor commandment has been put alongside of the *Shema* (Deut. 6:5), which every Jew was expected to recite every day.

Proper 26 (Closest to November 2)

A

Theme: Beware of irresponsible leaders.

Psalm 43

This third of a three-stanza poem (Pss. 42-43) is a prayer to God for defense and deliverance from deceitful and wicked men. The worshipper's soul is heavy because of them, yet his trust in God does not waver.

Micah 3:5-15

In the course of his oracles of ethical concern, Micah speaks out against immoral leaders. He condemns the prophets who falsely tailor their message to their own selfish interests rather than being motivated by the power of the Spirit. He also condemns the rulers of the people who pervert justice.

I Thessalonians 2:9-13, 17-20

Paul is usually thought of as a great evangelist and a profound theologian. Here we can sense another side of him: his deep pastoral concern for the people of the church he founded in Thessalonica.

Matthew 23:1-12

Jesus warns the crowds and his disciples not to follow the examples of the scribes and Pharisees. They do not practice what they preach, their behavior is ostentatious—not humble—and they look for honor and reward. All this is the opposite of what religious leaders should do and be. Like the prophets before him, Jesus condemns those leaders of the people who through selfishness lead God's people astray.

Proper 27 (Closest to November 9)

A

Theme: The coming day of the Lord

Psalm 70

Heard on this day, we identify the psalmist's prayer for deliverance with the coming day of the Lord. The psalmist sees that day as a time for which he longs and prays.

Amos 5:18-24

The central part of this book is a series of sermons of doom. Here the prophet speaks out against the casual readiness of worshippers who would treat God like one of themselves and forget both his sovereign majesty and his unequivocal demand for justice and right dealings. The coming day of the Lord cannot be anticipated lightly.

I Thessalonians 4:13-18
Paul and his colleagues believed profoundly in the early return of the Lord. The question had been raised as to the state of those believers who had died before Christ returned. This is his answer: they will share equally with those who are still alive.

Matthew 25:1-13
The parable of the wise and foolish bridesmaids is a warning to the disciples to be prepared and ready to enter the kingdom when the Lord comes. The oil is a symbol for repentance.

(Lead in: *"Jesus said, 'Then the kingdom of heaven. . . .' "*)

Proper 28 (Closest to November 16)

A

Theme: Prepare for the coming day of the Lord.

Psalm 90 [at the Eucharist:vss. 1-8, 12]
This older person is deeply conscious of the eternal being of God. He looks back over his long life with unflinching seriousness. Such a one is prepared for the coming day of the Lord.

Zephaniah 1:7, 12-18
This prophet is an inheritor of the moral concern of Amos and Isaiah. God is uncompromisingly holy, just, and righteous. The coming day of the Lord will be one of judgment against those who do not measure up. Here he speaks out against those who are indifferent or skeptical (v.12). By his extreme description of that day, he is saying that the Lord's coming cannot be taken lightly or shrugged off as of no consequence.

I Thessalonians 5: 1-10
The coming of the day of the Lord was as ominous to believers in the risen Lord as it was to Old Testament prophets, but with this difference: "God has not destined us for wrath, but to obtain salvation through our Lord Jesus Christ, who died for us" (vss. 9-10).

Matthew 25:14-15, 19-29
The parable of the talents is one of Jesus' parables of judgment. Readiness for the day of the Lord's coming is an active condition, involving work. And this will be the judgment: Those who make faithful use of the Lord's gifts will enter the life of the age to come; those who do

not, will not.

(Lead in: *"Jesus said, 'For it will be as. . . .'"*)

Proper 29 (Closest to November 23)

A

Theme: The coming encounter with the eternal Judge

Psalm 95:1-7

This portion of the psalm is a preparation of the people for their impending encounter with God.

Ezekiel 34:11-17

The whole chapter is about the shepherds of Israel and their sheep. Here God, through his prophet, describes himself as the good shepherd. He exercises more than tender care; the encounter with him also involves judgment.

1 Corinthians 15:20-28

In the course of his chapter about the resurrection of the dead, Paul has this paragraph regarding the order of events in the eschatological drama at the end of time, when history is rolled up. All things are subjected to the Son, who in the other readings on this day we know to be the eternal Judge. Then finally everything is subjected to God.

Matthew 25:31-46

In the parable of the last judgment, Jesus says that the ultimate distinction between persons will be whether one has or has not shown mercy to the oppressed. That emphasis can be traced all the way through Matthew's Gospel, making this parable, in a sense, a summary of the whole; and in Jesus' crucifixion and death we see "the King" identifying himself with the oppressed.

(Lead in: *"Jesus said, 'When the Son of man comes. . . .'"*)

The Sunday Lectionary

Year B

First Sunday of Advent

B

Theme: We look for the coming of our Savior and Judge.

Psalm 80 [at the Eucharist: vss. 1-7]
This psalm was a community lament probably at the time of an enemy invasion. When we hear these words our Christmas-oriented thoughts find an appropriateness in their yearning for the coming of the Lord who has the power to save.

Isaiah 64:1-9a
The original occasion for this ancient prayer is not as important as the fact that it sets the tone of our thinking as Advent begins. Here is yearning that God come among us and confession of sin that we may be fit to stand before him.

I Corinthians 1:1-9
The opening paragraph of this epistle puts us on our mettle. The faithful God has given us the grace of our Lord Jesus Christ so that we may not be "lacking in any spiritual gift." So we "wait for the revealing of our Lord Jesus Christ," whom we are confident will "sustain us to the end." How appropriate this is as Christmas draws near.

Mark 13: [24-32] 33-37
The Advent preparation for Christ's coming is twofold: his coming long ago into history—the nativity of Jesus—and his coming at the end of history "to judge the living and the dead." This Marcan passage warns us that we do not know when that second coming will be; therefore, we should always live worthily and expectantly.
(Lead in: *"Jesus said, 'But in those days. . . .'"*)

Second Sunday of Advent

B

Theme: We look for the coming salvation of the Lord.

Psalm 85 [at the Eucharist:vss. 7-13]
This psalm of comfort and hope contains both the yearning for the salvation of the Lord (v.7) and the promise that that divine blessing will shortly come to God's people (v.9). It is of a piece with the yearning and expectancy which run through the Advent season.

Isaiah 40:1-11
Second Isaiah contains the writings of a great unknown poet and some

lesser ones. His book (Isa. 40-66) opens with this poem, which could bear the title "The Coming of the Lord." Historically, the occasion was probably the end of the Babylonian exile, but these words are associated in our minds with John the Baptist and the coming of the Lord.

II Peter 3:8-15a, 18

The second-century Christian Church thought that the second coming of Christ, the righteous Judge, was very near. We may or may not share their view, but the season of Advent causes us to consider seriously "what sort of persons ought we to be in lives of holiness and godliness" (v.11).

Mark 1:1-8

John the Baptist heralded the coming of Christ, as the prophet foretold (Mal. 4:5-6). Here is Mark's terse account of the ministry of this forerunner of Jesus. Other Gospels contain more extended accounts of John's work and its meaning (Mt. 3:1-17; Lk. 3:1-20; Mt. 11:7-15; Jn. 1:6-8, 19-28).

Third Sunday of Advent

B

Theme: Prepare for the coming of the Savior.

Psalm 126

This psalm has been called "a precious stone in a simple and yet worthy setting" (Weiser). Originally, it probably reflected the religious community's expectation of salvation in a time of adversity. That expectation of salvation is set in a more majestic key as we look forward to the coming of the Savior of the world at Christmas.

Alternate to the Psalm: The Magnificat [Canticle 3 or 15]

This song of Mary was a part of her response when she learned that she was to be the mother of the Savior.

Isaiah 65:17-25

The prophet looks forward to the coming, final day of the Lord. The glorious new heaven and new conditions on earth will be related to the day when all men will acknowledge God as Lord. The Christian associates all this with the second coming of Christ.

(Lead in: *"Thus says the Lord God, 'For behold. . . .'"*)

I Thessalonians 5: [12-15] 16-28

In Paul's earliest writings it is evident that Christians lived in tiptoe expectancy of the imminent return of their Lord. Their attitude and consequent behavior is that to which we aspire as we prepare for Christmas.

John 1:6-8, 19-28 or John 3:23-30

We know something about John the Baptist from secular historical sources. This material is only hinted at in the Gospel records, for those writers were only interested in John as the forerunner of Jesus who prepared for his coming.

Fourth Sunday of Advent

B

Theme: The Son of David will shortly come.

Psalm 132 [at the Eucharist: vss. 8-15]

This psalm had some part in the festival of the enthronement of the king. Its appropriateness lies in the words, "The Lord has sworn an oath to David. . . of the fruit of your body will I set upon your throne" (vss. 11-12). We are about to celebrate the coming of the messianic Son of David.

II Samuel 7:4, 8-16

Through Nathan the prophet God tells David that he is destined to be king of the people of Israel and head of a royal line. Generations later Jesus was known as the Son of David (Matt. 12:22-23; 22:41-42).

(Lead in: *"The word of God came to Nathan. . . ."*)

Romans 16:25-27

The ascription with which the Epistle to the Romans ends has a Christmas ring to it: "kept secret for long ages but it is now disclosed. . . made known to all nations."

Luke 1:26-38

The angel's appearance to Mary is obviously appropriate here on the eve of Christmas. He is the Son of David, "and the Lord will give to him the throne of his father David" (v.32). The annunciation has been the subject of many great works of art.

Christmas Day, First Proper

B

Theme: Christ the Savior is born.

Psalm 96 [at the Eucharist: vss. 1-4, 11-12]

For the Christian, almost every verse of this psalm has to do with the Savior's birth.

Isaiah 9:2-4, 6-7

The prophet wrote this poem about the Messiah who was to come. It is impossible to read it without seeing in it a full-blown description of our Lord and his mission.

Titus 2:11-14

This epistle, written perhaps one hundred years after the crucifixion-resurrection, contains practical advice to leaders in the early Church. This section is particularly appropriate on Christmas Day.

Luke 2:1-14 [15-20]

This wonderful prose-poetry gives us the unforgettable picture of the nativity. The angel's announcement is for all time the classic statement of the Good News.

Christmas Day, Second Proper

B

Theme: Christ the Lord has come.

Psalm 97 [at the Eucharist: vss. 1-2, 8-12]

The special character of this psalm "allows an insight into the depth and comprehension of the Old Testament idea of the kingdom of God" (Weiser). This is appropriate at the celebration of the birth of him who ushered in that kingdom.

Isaiah 62:6-7, 10-12

Chapter 62 describes in a poem the people of God, the messianic people. In the first of the two stanzas we hear, the people are in tiptoe expectancy. The second depicts that people when the Messiah (Greek, Christ) has come.

Titus 3:4-7

This advice to early Christian leaders becomes an appropriate sermonette when we hear it on this day.

Luke 2: [1-14], 15-20

Our whole Biblical memory of Christmas centers in the angelic announcement to the shepherds and their visit to the manger Babe.

Christmas Day, Third Proper

B

Theme: The Word has become flesh and dwells among us.

Psalm 98 [at the Eucharist: vss. 1-6]

All creation is exhorted (vss. 7-9), along with God's people, to sing of the marvelous things God has done (v.1). Our reason for this song of joy is that God's righteousness has been "openly showed in the sight of the nations" (v.3) in the person of Jesus Christ.

Isaiah 52:7-10

These glorious verses are from a poem which might be entitled "The Lord Has Become King" (51:17-52:12). Here the arrival of the bearer of good news is described in unforgettable words.

Hebrews 1:1-12

This first chapter of Hebrews describes the incarnation of God's Son in terms of its eternal significance.

John 1:1-14

The Fourth Gospel opens, as does the Epistle to the Hebrews, with a description of the coming of God's Son from the point of view of God's eternal purpose and of man's response. The meaning of "Word" is pivotal. It embraces God's creative power, his purpose, his wisdom and his providence.

First Sunday after Christmas

B

Theme: God's grace is manifested in Jesus Christ.

Psalm 147 [at the Eucharist: vss. 13-21]

This psalm contains the essence of Hebrew worship. God is praised because of his power and because of "his compassionate grace as manifested in creation and election"(Weiser). But with the coming of Jesus Christ, God's grace has been set in a higher key.

Isaiah 61:10-62:3

In some of the most stirring poetry of the Bible an ancient seer sings of the glad tidings of salvation to Zion. Heard on this day these words become part of the profound joy of this feast of Christ's nativity.

Galatians 3:23-25; 4:4-7

With the coming of Christ, man's relation to God has changed radically from legalism to faith. Paul explains that the discipline of trying to keep the law was the training that prepares us for faith in Christ's merciful power. The emphasis has changed from seeking to gain God's favor by the good works we do putting our faith in his love for us. It is the difference between a slave and an adopted son.

John 1:1-18

The prologue of John's Gospel also makes clear the point of the Galatians passage above. "The law was given through Moses; grace and truth came through Jesus Christ" (v.17). "Grace" here means undeserved, unexpected kindness and caring.

Holy Name, January 1

B

Theme: Hallowed by thy Name.

Psalm 8

In the refrain with which this psalm opens and closes, God's Name is the revelation of his nature. The intervening verses expand on this, ringing with fear and joy, thus blending the two opposite fundamental religious attitudes.

Exodus 34:1-8

The earlier part of this narrative described the giving of the Ten Commandments, the impatient people worshipping the golden calf, and Moses breaking the tablets on which the Commandments were written (Exod. 32). Now Moses goes up the mountain a second time to receive the Commandments from God. He proclaims the Name of the Lord in the words of the old liturgical confession which is often repeated throughout the O.T. (II Chron. 30:9; Neh. 9:17, 31; Joel 2:13; Jonah 4:2; Ps. 86:15; etc.). (Note: in v. 5 most commentators designate Moses as the subject of the verb "stood." The reading becomes clearer if this is done.)

Romans 1:1-7

The salutation with which Paul's epistle opens indicates the motive which inspired his mission. Through Jesus Christ our Lord "we have received grace (power) and apostleship to bring about obedience to the faith for the sake of his name among all nations" (v.5). This passage lies behind Edward Perronet's hymn "All hail the power of Jesus' Name!"

Luke 2:15-21

This is the account of the naming of Jesus in the nativity story. The name Jesus means "Yahweh is salvation." He was given this name because "he will save his people from their sins" (Mt. 1:21).

Second Sunday after Christmas

B

Theme: Pilgrims all/The pilgrimage of God's people.

Psalm 84 [at the Eucharist: vss. 1-8]
This is a pilgrims' song. "Happy are the people. . .whose hearts are set on the pilgrims' way" (v.4). This could once have been sung by the Holy Family as they journeyed to the feast of Jerusalem or, in essence, been the sentiment of Wise Men as they journeyed.

Jeremiah 31:7-14
Within Jeremiah's book is a little Book of Comfort (chaps. 30-31). This portion of it describes in a poem the return to Zion of exiles from all nations.

Ephesians 1:3-6, 15-19a
The writer begins his epistle with thanksgiving for the receipt of "every spiritual blessing in the heavenly places" (v.3) by the Ephesians, whom he describes as "having the eyes of your heart enlightened" (v.18). They had made a spiritual pilgrimage.

Matthew 2:13-15, 19-23
This is the account of the flight of the Holy Family into Egypt to avoid the wrath of King Herod, and of their ultimate return to Galilee and the city of Nazareth, where Jesus grew up.

Alternate Gospel: Luke 2:41-52
The only boyhood story about Jesus is this account of what happened when he and his family made the pilgrimage to Jerusalem at Passover time.

Alternate Gospel: Matthew 2:1-12
The story of the Wise Men coming to worship the Christ Child is a beloved part of the Christmas sequence. The major theme of Matthew's Gospel is that the Jews rejected the offered salvation but the Gentiles accepted it. This story introduces that theme. While this reading anticipates the Feast of the Epiphany, where it properly belongs, it is also appropriate here, since the Wise Men were making a religious pilgrimage.

The Epiphany, January 6

B

Theme: All the earth will come and worship him.

Psalm 72 [at the Eucharist: vss. 1-2, 10-17]

Some scholars have interpreted this psalm as referring to the Messiah. Its appropriateness in this feast lies in the fact that the psalmist foresaw that kings of other lands would bow down before him (vss. 10-11, 15).

Isaiah 60:1-6, 9

The prophet assures the Babylonian exiles that God will save and restore his people. This will be witnessed by the nations, who therefore come and worship the Savior God. The passage puts into poetry the message of the story of the Wise Men.

Ephesians 3:1-12

The theme of this epistle is that all people find their unity in Christ. So the writer logically holds the conviction that "Gentiles are fellow heirs, members of the same body, and partakers of the promise in Christ Jesus through the gospel" (v.6).

Matthew 2:1-12

The story of the Wise Men sets forth the Epiphany message in picture pageantry: Christ is recognized by representatives of the nations who come to worship him.

First Sunday after the Epiphany

B

Theme: The baptism of Jesus

Psalm 89:1-29 [at the Eucharist: vss. 20-29]

This long psalm is a lament at the time of some great national disaster. The first of its three parts (vss. 1-18) is a hymn of praise to God. The opening section of part two (vss. 19-29) deals with the great promises made to King David. When we hear them on this day we identify them with Jesus at the time of his baptism.

Isaiah 42:1-9

On this day when we celebrate Jesus' baptism this "servant poem" from Second Isaiah is most appropriate. Regardless of whom the poet had in mind, the Christian identifies the Lord's servant with Jesus. "He is my chosen, in whom my soul delights; I have put my spirit upon him" (v.1).

Acts 10:34-38

Peter addresses the Roman centurion Cornelius and his family, who were eager to be baptized, Peter's description of Jesus gives prominence to his baptism: "anointed by God with the Holy Spirit and with power." (v.38)

Mark 1: 7-11

The baptism of Jesus is an ancient Epiphany season theme. It is central to the teaching of the season: Jesus Christ is manifested to the world as God's Son.

(Lead in: *"John the Baptizer appeared in the wilderness and preached, saying. . ."*)

Second Sunday after the Epiphany

B

Theme: The call of the Lord

Psalm 63:1-8

This is in a sense the meditation of one who stands in God's presence in the sanctuary. It might also be thought of as the set of mind of those who hear and obey the call of the Lord.

I Samuel 3:1-10 [11-20]

The boy Samuel is called by God to be his prophet, and a new day dawns in the life of the people of Israel.

I Corinthians 6:11b-20

The apostle is speaking to a problem in the Church of another day. Yet, heard in a culture where drugs and alcohol, exercise, and dieting play a prominent part, his counsel still applies: "Glorify God in your body, for it is a temple of the Holy Spirit" (vss. 19, 20).

John 1:43-51

The Lord calls Phillip and Nathanael to be his disciples.

Third Sunday after the Epiphany

B

Theme: Repent, that the Lord may forgive.

Psalm 130

This is one of the major penitential psalms of the ancient Church. The God-fearing person who composed it had a deep understanding of the nature of sin and of divine forgiveness.

Jeremiah 3:21-4:2

Early in his ministry the prophet issues this summons to genuine repentance.

I Corinthians 7:17-23

In a section of his epistle which is filled with advice to fellow Christians, the apostle makes it clear that one's status in the world is not of primary importance so far as being a servant of the Lord is concerned. That which counts is "keeping the commandments of God" (v.19).

Mark 1:14-20

Here is a glimpse of the very beginning of Jesus' ministry. It may be coincidence, but Jesus, who was steeped in the writings of the prophets, began his ministry with a call to repentance, just as Jeremiah had done before him.

Fourth Sunday after the Epiphany

B

Theme: The spokesmen of the Lord

Psalm 111

The psalmist tells us exultantly what God means to him. Those who "fear the Lord" (v.10) are likely to have a deep appreciation of the word as it comes to us from his special agents.

Deuternomy 18:15-20

This is the only passage in the Law (the first five books) which establishes prophecy as an institution (*The Interpreter's Bible*). Its significance here is that the prophet is one to whom the Lord reveals his will and who speaks that which he is commanded.

(Lead in: *"Moses summoned all Israel and said to them, 'The Lord your God. . . .' "*)

I Corinthians 8:1b-13

Paul is dealing with a religious problem of first century Christians: eating food which has been offered to idols. The principle which he enunciates throws revealing light on the observance of the Golden Rule.

Mark 1:21-28

Early in Jesus' ministry people began to recognize that what he said and did demonstrated an innate authority other religious teachers lacked. In Mark's Gospel the unclean spirits realized who Jesus was long before his disciples did.

(Lead in: *"Jesus and his disciples came to Capernaum, and immediately on the sabbath he entered. . . ."*)

Fifth Sunday after the Epiphany

B

Theme: God is a present help in trouble.

Psalm 142
This is the prayer of lament of one who has been forsaken. Whatever the psalmist's dire circumstance, it is his attitude of mind and deep trust in God which gives his words their distinct character.

II Kings 4: [8-17] 18-21 [22-31] 32-37
This is one of the wonder stories in the Elisha saga. Whatever may be the facts, Israel's memory of Elisha was that of a man of God with whose name many wonderful happenings became associated.

(Lead in when the reading begins with v.18: *"When the son of the Shunammite woman had grown. . . ."*)

I Corinthians 9:16-23
Again and again the Bible pictures men under compulsion to be God's agents and messengers. Amos is one (3:8); Jeremiah is another (20:9). Here Paul writes that he *must* proclaim the Gospel, the story of God's love as revealed in Christ. This same imperative comes to every Christian. Some hear it more clearly than others.

Mark 1:29-39
This little vignette from a typical day in our Lord's early ministry gives us a glimpse of some of the immeasurable riches people receive from the presence and power of Christ.

(Lead in: *"Immediately Jesus left the synagogue. . . ."*)

Sixth Sunday after the Epiphany

B

Theme: Lepers are healed by the power of God.

Psalm 42 [at the Eucharist: vss. 1-7]
The two stanzas of this poem (Ps.43 is the third) are the moving words of a sufferer. He yearns to be able once again to worship in the temple of God, whom he recognizes as his unfailing source of help.

II Kings 5:1-15ab [end with the word "Israel."]
The healing of Naaman the leper is part of the saga of Elisha, the man of God.

I Corinthians 9:24-27

In a longer section on the nature of the Christian's freedom (8:1-11:1) the apostle includes this nugget on the importance of self-discipline. Righteous living requires the same serious effort as that of the runner who must constantly keep in training in order to run a good race.

Mark 1:40-45

This account of Jesus healing a leper is one of many incidents remembered about Jesus and recorded because it reveals the power of God to save.

(Lead in: *"A leper came to Jesus. . . ."*)

Seventh Sunday after the Epiphany

B

Theme: The forgiving God is faithful.

Psalm 32 [at the Eucharist: vss. 1-8]

In this psalm of thanksgiving the poet thinks back on his penitence and God's forgiveness. This is the reason for his present joy.

Isaiah 43:18-25

Throughout the stirring poetry of Second Isaiah runs the conviction that God, the Holy One of Israel, genuinely cares about his chosen people. It is evident here in giving water in the desert. But Israel is unfaithful: "I have not burdened you (with ritualistic observances)," God says, "But you have burdened me with your sins" (vss.23-24). Yet God continues to be true to his nature—the Holy One who forgives "for my own sake" (v.25).

II Corinthians 1:18-22

The forgiving God is faithful: he does not vacillate between Yes and No (vss. 17 and 19). And Paul's conviction that "all the promises of God find their YES in Jesus Christ" (v.20) causes us to re-read the Gospel story with new appreciation.

Mark 2:1-12

In the time of Jesus affliction was thought to be evidence of sin, and healing was closely associated with forgiveness. People found that when they were in the presence of Jesus, God's forgiveness was undeniably real.

Eighth Sunday after the Epiphany

B

Theme: Forget not his benefits.

Psalm 103 [at the Eucharist: vss. 1-6]

Here is a jubilant song in praise of God's fatherly love, one of the finest in the Psalter. "Forget not all his benefits," (v.2) the psalmist counsels, and then enumerates a number of those benefits.

Hosea 2:14-23

Israel, because of her apostasy, is considered an unfaithful wife whom God is willing to take back and to whom he will become re-betrothed. The warmth of divine compassion is one of the benefits from the Lord of which we ought to be continually mindful. (Note: Jezreel - "God sows" - was the name given Israel in her apostasy; once a name of judgment, now it is a name of promise. Read "God sows" and the meaning is clear without explanation.)

(Lead in: *"The Lord said to Hosea, 'Behold. . . .' "*)

II Corinthians 3: [4-11] 17-4:2

The risen Lord who first appeared to the apostle on the Damascus road is his inspiration and motivating force. The presence of this risen Lord is the Holy Spirit (3:18), and this Spirit gives life. The conviction of this sufficiency carries with it a great sense of freedom. In his way Paul is saying, "Know the truth and the truth will make you free" (Jn.8:32).

Mark 2:18-22

Being with Jesus turned his disciples' lives around. Their resulting behavior, as well as his words, created the opposition to Jesus which ultimately brought him to the cross. Jesus still turns lives around. When we are alive to his presence, we are alive to his benefits.

Last Sunday after the Epiphany

B

Theme: The transfiguration of Christ.

Psalm 27 [at the Eucharist: vss. 1-9]

Here are two psalms in one—vss.1-8, a hymn of faith, and vss.9-17, the prayer of one in need of help. In the course of the first we find the words, "to behold the fair beauty of the Lord" (v.5), which might call to mind the transfiguration.

I Kings 19:9-18

Elijah, the beleaguered, lonely prophet, finds himself in God's presence on a mountainside. He is told what he is to do next and that he is not alone in God's service.

(Lead in: *"On Horeb, the mount of God, Elijah came to a cave. . ."*)

II Peter 1:16-19 [20-21]

The transfiguration of Jesus on the mountain is told in each of the first three Gospels and here in this epistle whose author was with Jesus on that occasion.

Mark 9:2-9

The transfiguration story describes the disciples' realization that their Lord had fulfilled their ancient religious tradition, which in their vision is represented by Moses and Elijah. This is a turning point in the Gospel record. From here on the center of interest is Jesus' approaching death.

First Sunday in Lent

B

Theme: The God of my salvation/Tempted by Satan

Psalm 25 [at the Eucharist: vss. 3-9]

This is the earnest prayer of a pious person. He appeals to "the God of my salvation" (v.4) in whom he hopes, and whom he trusts for protection and deliverence (vv. 19-20).

Genesis 9:8-17

A foundation stone of Biblical religion is God's covenant with Israel (cf. Gen. 17:7), God saves Noah from the flood waters and the rainbow is the sign of the covenant of this saving God with his people.

I Peter 3:18-22

A central element in Christian baptism is that the crucified and risen Lord who is "alive in the spirit" (v.18) bestows his Spirit on the believer. Water and the Spirit are inseparably associated in baptism (Jn. 3:5). The waters from which Noah was saved become here the water through which the Christian believer is saved in baptism.

Mark 1:9-13

Mark's account of Jesus' temptations in the wilderness after his baptism is terse: "tempted by Satan" forty days, but obviously to no avail for then "the angels ministered to him." The comforting and reassuring description of him in later years was "tempted as we are, yet without sin." (Heb. 4:15). This is the beloved Son who calls disciples—then and now.

Second Sunday in Lent

B

Theme: The faith and commitment of those who belong to the Lord

Psalm 16 [at the Eucharist: vss. 5-11]

This psalm, which is in part set in the form of a prayer, is an affirmation of trust in God. The psalmist sums up his wholehearted commitment to the Lord with the words, "I have set the Lord always before me" (v.8).

Genesis 22:1-14

Abraham is known as the father of the faithful as much for this incident as for any other. He had utter faith both in God's goodness and in his promise that one day Abraham's descendants would be a great nation.

Romans 8:31-39

Just as Abraham's faith is a major part of our religious heritage, so also is Paul's great faith that nothing can separate us from the love of Christ.

Mark 8:31-38

In our Lord's teaching the road to salvation involves an all-out commitment. "Whoever would save his life will lose it." Halfway measures of doing or believing will not suffice.

(Lead in: *"Jesus began to teach them. . . ."*)

Third Sunday in Lent

B

Theme: God's law/The desecrated temple

Psalm 19:7-14

Psalm 19 is two separate psalms; the second half, which we have here, is a hymn in praise of God's law.

Exodus 20:1-17

The Ten Commandments are thought of as the epitome and symbol of God's will for his people. The giving of the commandments to Moses on Mt. Sinai is a milestone event in Israel's salvation history.

Romans 7:13-25

This is Paul's psychological analysis of sin. The law makes us conscious of what we should do, but in each of us there is "another law at war with the law of my mind" (v.23). It is through faith in Jesus Christ that one can be saved from this dilemma.

John 2:13-22

The trading which went on in the outer court of the temple took place because pilgrim worshippers who had come to celebrate the Passover needed to buy sacrificial animals. Symbolically, Jesus was overthrowing the old religious system and replacing it with faith in him. Then, he turned the discussion into a prediction of his coming death and resurrection.

Fourth Sunday in Lent

B
Theme: The gracious God is Lord over the events of history/He feeds his people.

Psalm 122
This psalm contains the fervent prayer for the peace of Jerusalem offered by those who love that city as the symbol of all they hold precious.

II Chronicles 36:14-23
One great evidence of the mighty hand of the Lord working in the history of Israel is described here in the summary at the end of Chronicles. Israel had flouted the will of the God of their fathers, so God caused them to be taken into exile. Then after an appropriate time, he caused Cyrus, king of Persia, to let them return and rebuild their homeland.

Ephesians 2:4-10
The author makes it clear that it is only by the graciousness of a compassionate God that we are saved. Christians know this because of the death and resurrection of Jesus Christ, but it has always been God's way with man.

John 6:4-15
This mid-Lent Sunday is sometimes called "Refreshment Sunday," partly in reference to this Gospel account of the great feeding and partly because this is a little recess from the stern practices of Lenten observance. This feeding takes on eternal signficance because of the death and resurrection of him who is the Bread of the World.

Fifth Sunday in Lent

B
Theme: The new heart of the forgiven penitent/The cross will draw all people to Christ.

Psalm 51 [at the Eucharist: vss. 11-16]
This greatest of the penitential psalms is appropriate here because in the

depths of his penitence the psalmist prays that God will "create in me a clean heart" (v.11).

Jeremiah 31:31-34
This is a fundamental O.T. passage which looks beyond the law of Moses to a new dispensation. It is quoted twice in Hebrews (8:8ff. and 10:16ff.) and lies behind Paul's thinking in II Corinthians 3:5-14. It is a high point of prophetic insight.

Hebrews 5: [1-4] 5-10
The new covenant of which the prophet spoke (Jer. 31:31-34) becomes possible not because of our good works but through the high priesthood of the risen and ascended Christ. This passage sets forth his qualification for that role, the chief of which is that he has been made perfect through suffering.

John 12:20-33
The coming of certain Greeks to worship Jesus is a foretaste of what was to be after his death and resurrection. The Father's Name will be glorified by his death, and "all men" will thus be drawn to the worship of God.

Palm Sunday

B

Theme: The passion of Jesus Christ

Psalm 22:1-21 [at the Eucharist: vss. 1-11]
The prayer of a lonely, put-upon individual opens with those familiar words quoted by Jesus during his desolate hours on the cross. The similarity between the sufferings of Jesus and those of the psalmist is striking.

Isaiah 45:21-25
These several stanzas are from a poem (vss. 14-25) concerning the conversation of the nations. In them God makes clear that he, the righteous God and Savior of "all the ends of the earth," will triumph.

Alternate reading: Isaiah 52:13-53:12
This last of the four "servant of the Lord" poems scattered through Isaiah from chapters 42 to 53 describes one who humbly accepts suffering on behalf of his people. Scholars do not agree as to whether the servant is an individual, a dedicated remnant of the people, or the whole nation of Israel. In any case, we think of this passage as one of the spiritual high points of the O.T. and see in it a description of the meaning of Christ's passion.

Philippians 2:5-11

Here in a nutshell is Paul's belief about Jesus Christ. He who humbled himself to become a man and to die on the cross is the Lord of all.

Mark [14:32-72;] 15:1-39 [40-47]

The passion and death of Jesus Christ as narrated by Mark.

Easter Day

B

Theme: The resurrection of Jesus Christ

Psalm 118:14-29 [at the Eucharist: vss. 14-17, 22-24]

This is the exultant hymn of those who have had a direct experience of the help of God. It is in two parts: the thanksgiving of an individual and the thanksgiving of a chorus of pilgrims. Here we have part of the thanksgiving of the individual (vss. 14-21) plus the thanksgiving of the chorus (vss. 22-29). In the context of Easter Day, we may picture the individual as the risen Christ and the chorus as his faithful believers.

Acts 10:34-43

Peter was the leader of the Twelve and the first to see the risen Lord (Lk. 24:34). Here is part of one of his early sermons, in which it is obvious that the resurrection of Christ is of crucial importance.

Alternate first reading: Isaiah 25:6-9

This little passage foretells God's victory: the feast of triumph and the end of sorrow. It certainly has Easter overtones when we hear it on this day.

Colossians 3:1-4

The conviction that the risen Lord has conquered both sin and death is intended to influence all that the Christian is and does.

Alternate Epistle: Acts 10:34-43 [see above]

Mark 16:1-8

Mark's account of what happened on the first Easter morning is the earliest and probably the least embellished. These are the words with which the Gospel ends. We sense the women's astonishment, awe, and fear at the discovery of the empty tomb.

Theme: The risen presence and the life of believers

Psalm 114
This is a hymn of praise to God because of the exodus, which is the fundamental saving act of the O.T. The Lord's resurrection is the fundamental saving act of God in the new covenant.

Alternate psalm: Psalm 136
This litany psalm bears witness to God's perpetual grace in creation and in history. A major event in that history is the exodus from Egypt (vss. 11-15), which is thought of as the O.T. counterpart of the resurrection.

Alternate psalm: Psalm 118:14-17, 22-24
This psalm is a powerful testimony to the strength of faith. The portion read here sounds like a hymn of thanksgiving for the Lord's resurrection.

Acts 5:29a, 30-32
This is Peter's witness to the resurrection before the Sanhedrin.

Alternate first reading: Daniel 12:1-3
The Book of Daniel ends with visions of the last days. There will be a time of general resurrection and judgment. This insight is reflected in the N.T. (Jn. 5:29 and Acts 24:15). One of God's great gifts is suggested here: the life that God has given each of us is precious, and he cares how we use it.

I Corinthians 5:6b-8
Leaven has an infectious quality and was usually considered a symbol of defilement. But it was also the sign of a new start, since its use meant that there was no sour dough left from a previous baking. In the Passover ritual unleavened bread was associated with the remembrance of Israel's redemption from Egypt—a people's new start. Here Paul transfers that ancient association to Christ's resurrection and the new start which is ours because of the risen Christ.

Alternate Epistle: Acts 5:29a, 30-32 [see above]

Luke 24:13-35
Luke's Easter evening account is significant because the ways in which those disciples knew the risen Lord are ways which are ours also: the opening of the Scriptures and the breaking of bread—Word and Sacrament.

Second Sunday of Easter

Theme: Belief in the resurrection is our salvation.

Psalm 111

In this hymn in praise of God's great acts, the psalmist describes more than he knows. The great deeds of the Lord (v.2), the splendor and power of his work (vss.3, 6), and the redemption he gives his people (v.9) can all be applied to Christ's resurrection.

Alternate psalm: Psalm 118:19-24

These words are an appropriate Easter psalm, for the Christian cannot hear them without thinking of Christ's resurrection.

Acts 3:12a, 13-15, 17-26

As Peter and John were entering the temple, they were accosted by a lame beggar. Instead of giving him alms, Peter healed him. A crowd immediately gathered. In answer to their wonderment, this is what Peter said.

(Lead in: start with v.11 thus, *"While the healed man clung to Peter and John. . ."*)

Alternate to the Acts reading: Isaiah 26:2-9, 19

These words are part of a longer poetic oracle (25:10-27:1). We associate the prophet's joyful words of thanksgiving for victory with the Lord's victorious resurrection, especially when he goes on to say, "Thy dead shall live, their bodies shall rise. . . sing for joy!" (v.19).

I John 5:1-6

Faith in the risen Lord is the means by which we overcome "the world," i.e., the power of the evil one, specifically sin and death (v.19). Hence belief in Christ's resurrection is our salvation.

Alternate Epistle: Acts 3:12a, 13-15, 17-26 [see above]

John 20:19-31

The earliest record of resurrection appearances is in I Corinthians 15:3-8. Those appearances fall into two categories. The first group (to Cephas or Peter *et al.*) has a church-founding significance. The second group (to James *et al.*) has a mission-inaugurating significance. The two appearances described in John 20 are in the first category. Jesus binds the disciples together in their conviction of his risen presence. The Holy Spirit is bestowed, and here is the beginning of the Church as a spiritual entity.

(Lead in: *"On the evening of Easter day. . . ."*)

Third Sunday of Easter

Theme: Witnesses to the resurrection

Psalm 98 [at the Eucharist: vss.1-5]
This joyful hymn is appropriate for those who go forth to bear witness to the good news of the Lord's resurrection. It *is* "a new song," for the Lord has "got for himself the victory," and he has made it known (vss.1-3).

Acts 4:5-12
When Peter and John went to the temple to pray, they were accosted at the gate by a lame beggar seeking alms. Instead, Peter healed him. In his explanation to the crowd that gathered, Peter explained that what had happened was a result of the resurrection of Jesus Christ. The religious authorities had them arrested. Here they make their defense before the Sanhedrin.

Alternate to the Acts reading: Micah 4:1-5
The prophet writes of his visions of a glorious future. In what was happening in Jerusalem in the days following the resurrection we see his words beginning to be fulfulled. "The word of the Lord (shall go forth) from Jerusalem," "and peoples shall flow to it" (vss.2,1; cf. Acts 3:11f.; 4:12f.).

I John 1:1-2:2
John makes clear at the beginning of his epistle that he is bearing witness to that which he knows first hand (vss. 1-3). The presence of the risen Lord is not a theory or something that happened in the past, but a present reality. This gives his words great immediacy and authority.

Alternate Epistle: Acts 4:5-12 [see above]

Luke 24:36b-48
In the final resurrection appearance of Jesus to the disciples before his ascension, he makes sure that there is no doubt in their minds that he is alive. Then he says to them, "You are witnesses of these things" (v.48).
(Lead in: *"While the disciples were talking, the risen Jesus himself. . . ."*)

Fourth Sunday of Easter

Theme: Good and bad shepherds

Psalm 23
The shepherd psalm is perhaps the best known of all the psalms.

Alternate Psalm: Psalm 100

This psalm, best known as *Jubilate Deo*, has as its keynote joy in the Lord, and it lifts the hearts of those who join in it. For us, God's shepherd-like concern for his people is part of that joy.

Acts 4:[23-31] 32-37

There were several distinctive marks of the early company of believers in the resurrection. They were bold and courageous witnesses to that which they knew firsthand—the risen presence of the Lord—and they had a genuine, brotherly concern for one another—a shepherd-like concern for the flock of Christ.

(Lead in: *"When Peter and John were released. . . ."*)

Alternate to the Acts reading: Ezekiel 34:1-10

God, speaking through his prophet, condemns the leaders of the people for their failure to have a shepherd-like interest in the welfare of his people. The Lord will himself be their good shepherd (vss. 11-12a).

I John 3:1-8

The Sunday-by-Sunday serial reading of this epistle continues. Here the writer is contrasting the children of God and the children of the evil one.

Alternate Epistle: Acts 4: [23-31] 32-37 [see above]

John 10:11-16

In the course of this chapter in which Jesus describes himself as the Good Shepherd, he contrasts his behavior and concern with that of the bad shepherd whom he calls "a hireling."

(Lead in: *"Jesus said, 'I am. . . .' "*)

Fifth Sunday of Easter

B

Theme: God's commandments

Psalm 66:1-11 [at the Eucharist: vss. 1-8]

This is a hymn of praise to God for his awesome and wonderful doings for the children of men (vss. 2 and 4).

Acts 8:26-40

This vividly-told account of Philip baptizing an Ethiopian eunuch (probably already a proselyte) is most significant because it is the first time the suffering servant passage in Isaiah 53 is quoted in Christian teaching. The incident shows that the Gospel is spreading. The Lord's command, "Go. . .make disciples of all nations, baptizing them. . ." (Mt.28:19), is being obeyed.

Alternate to the Acts reading: Deuteronomy 4:32-40
This is Moses' strong argument to the Israelites as to the importance of keeping God's commandments. He enumerates all the unusual and undeserved things God has done for Israel; then he says, "Therefore, keep the commandments." Keeping the commandments is our response, our acts of gratitude for what God has done for us.
(Lead in: *"Moses said, 'For ask now. . . .'"*)

I John 3: [14-17] 18-24
In the course of his description of the children of God, John adds details to the meaning of the Lord's "new commandment—that you love one another" (Jn.13:34).

Alternate Epistle: Acts 8:26-40 [see above]

John 14:15-21
Keeping the Lord's commandments is evidence of love for God in Christ.
(Lead in: *"Jesus said, 'If you love me. . . .'"*)

Sixth Sunday of Easter

B

Theme: Love one another.

Psalm 33 [at the Eucharist: vss.1-8, 18-22]
The "new song" celebrated on this day is the realization of the early Christian that all peoples are included in God's salvation history and hence, through his witnesses, "the loving-kindness of the Lord fills the whole earth" (v.5).

Acts 11:19-30
The risen Christ had appeared only to Jews, but slowly the realization came that the good news of the cross and resurrection is for all people. This account reflects that dawning awareness. Gradually the apostles realized that "Love one another" also includes Gentiles.
(Lead in: *"Now the believers in the risen Lord who were. . . ."*)

Alternate to the Acts reading: Isaiah 45:11-13, 18-19
These stanzas from the poetry of Second Isaiah make it clear that God is Lord over nature, which he intended for man to use to his glory. This reading is appropriate here on the eve of the Rogation Days, when we ask God's blessing on our plantings.

I John 4:7-21

In the continuing serial reading of this epistle, we come to this discussion of "Love one another." The second part of Jesus' summary of the Law lays down the principle (Mk.12:31, cf. Lev.19:18), the parable of the Good Samaritan makes it graphic (Lk.10:29f), and here John probes the depths of its meaning.

Alternate Epistle: Acts 11:19-30 [see above]

John 15:9-17

Here is that section of the Lord's upper room discourse in which he discusses "Love one another."

(Lead in: *"Jesus said: 'As the Father. . . .' "*)

Seventh Sunday of Easter

B

Theme: Christ the eternal high priest

Psalm 68:1-20

This is a complicated, involved psalm. It deals in part with the response of the praying community to the revelation of God. On this Sunday following the ascension it seems especially appropriate because of such expressions as, "Magnify him who rides upon the heavens" (v.4), and "You have gone up on high" (v.18).

Alternate psalm: Psalm 47

A part of the thinking about Christ's ascension is that he is enthroned in heaven and recognized as Lord of all. This is a major theme in Ascensiontide hymns. This psalm depicts the enthronement of God: "God has gone up with a shout." He "sits upon his holy throne" and is "king of all the earth" (vss. 5, 6, 8).

Acts 1:15-26

Here is Luke's account of what took place during the ten days between the Lord's ascension and the coming of the Spirit on the Day of Pentecost.

Alternate to the Acts reading: Exodus 28:1-4, 9-10, 29-30

This is a description of the beginning of the ancient high priesthood on the traditions of Israel. The high priest's vocation was that of interceding for Israel before God. The risen Christ, having ascended into the heavens, is the eternal high priest ever interceding for us (Heb.4:14-15; 7:23-25; and Rom. 8:34).

(Lead in: *"Moses said, 'These are. . . .' "*)

I John 5:9-15

This is the last in the series of readings from I John. "He who has the Son has life" (v.12). This, in a sense, has been the theme of John's epistle, and now he drives home its importance.

Alternate to the Epistle: Acts 1:15-26 [see above]

John 17:11b-19

This is part of the high-priestly prayer of Jesus for his disciples shortly before his passion. Here he is interceding for them, an activity which is germane to the role of high priest.

(Lead in: *"Jesus prayed, 'Now I am. . . .' "*)

Day of Pentecost

B

Theme: The gift of the Spirit

Psalm 104:25-37 [at the Eucharist: vss. 25, 28-31]

This psalm is one of the most beautiful poems in the Psalter. The first half is in effect the Genesis creation story set to music. This latter portion is chiefly in praise of God the preserver of life. The creedal phrase, "the Lord, and Giver of Life," has some of its O.T. roots here.

Alternate psalm at the Eucharist: Psalm 33:12-15, 18-22

These verses of this Covenant Festival hymn express abounding joy because God is favorably disposed toward his people. This same attitude of heart and mind is characteristic of the celebration of the Christian Pentecost.

Acts 2:1-11

The first Christian Pentecost occurred on the ancient Jewish feast of that name, fifty days after that Feast of the Passover during which the crucifixion took place. This day was the occasion on which the believers in the risen Lord first became aware of the presence of God's Spirit in their midst. Pentecost marks the beginning of the dynamic missionary life of the Christian Church.

Alternate to the Acts reading: Isaiah 44:1-8

Here are stanzas about what God is doing for his people. When we hear them on Pentecost they have meaning far beyond that intended by the unknown poet who lived in the middle of the sixth century B.C.: "I will pour my Spirit upon your descendants, and my blessing on your offspring" (v.3).

I Corinthians 12:4-13
The gift of the Spirit is evident in God's people in a variety of ways.

Alternate to the Epistle: Acts 2:1-11 [see above]

John 20:19-23
Here the risen Lord bestows his Holy Spirit on his disciples. In the Luke-Acts tradition this occurred on a separate occasion, not during one of the resurrection appearances (Acts 2:1-11).
(Lead in: *"On the evening of Easter day. . . ."*)

Alternate Gospel: John 14:8-17
This part of Jesus' upper room discourse is appropriate on Pentecost because it throws light on the nature and function of the Holy Spirit.

Trinity Sunday (First Sunday after Pentecost):

Theme: The presence of the holy God

Psalm 93
This is a hymn about the majesty of God.

Alternate to the psalm: Benedictus es, Domine [Canticle 2 or 13]
This hymn in praise of the God of our fathers is from the "Song of the Three Holy Children" in the Aprocrypha and is familiar to us as one of the Morning Prayer canticles. It conveys a deep sense of the majesty and splendor of God.

Exodus 3:1-6
Moses at the burning bush was in the presence of the God of his fathers. God's presence is frequently identified with fire or brightness in the Bible. (Exod. 13:21; 19:18; 33:11; 34:29 are a few examples.)

Romans 8:12-17
The Spirit of God is identified with both the Father and Christ. This line of thought led in time to the doctrine of the Trinity.

John 3:1-16
Interwoven in Jesus' conversation with Nicodemus and the subsequent discourse is the truth that God the Father, the Son, and the Spirit are inseparably one.

The Season after Pentecost

Directions for the use of the Propers which follow are on page vi of the Introduction.

Proper 1 (Closest to May 11)

B

Theme: Lepers are healed by the power of God.

Psalm 42 [at the Eucharist: vss. 1-7]
The two stanzas of this poem (Ps. 43 is the third) are the moving words of a sufferer. Here is the attitude of mind of those who know they have been healed by the power of God.

II Kings 5:1-15ab [end with the word "Israel."]
The healing of Naaman the leper is part of the saga of Elisha, the man of God.

I Corinthians 9:24-27
In a longer section about the nature of the Christian's freedom (8:1-11:1) the apostle includes this nugget on the importance of self-discipline. Righteous living requires the same serious effort as that of the runner who must constantly keep in training in order to run a good race.

Mark 1:40-45
This account of Jesus healing a leper is one of many incidents remembered about Jesus and recorded because it reveals the power of God to save.

Proper 2 (Closest to May 18)

B

Theme: The Lord cares and forgives and heals.

Psalm 32 [at the Eucharist: vss. 1-8]
In this psalm of thanksgiving the poet thinks back on his penitence and God's forgiveness. This is the reason for his present joy.

Isaiah 43:15-21
Throughout the stirring poetry of Second Isaiah runs the conviction that God, the Holy One of Israel, cares deeply for his chosen people. This is evident here in giving water in the desert.

II Corinthians 1:18-22
Sometimes comments made almost in an offhand way open new vistas of thought to their hearers. When Paul writes that "all the promises of God

find their YES in Jesus Christ" (v.20), it is time to go back and reread the Gospel story with new appreciation.

Mark 2:1-12

This snapshot of the teaching-healing ministry of Jesus shows how very much he cared about people. Surely the heavenly Father's loving concern—his caring—is as great as that which people experienced when they came to Jesus (cf. Jer. 30:17).

Proper 3 (Closest to May 25)

B

Theme: Forget not his benefits.

Psalm 103 [at the Eucharist: vss.1-6]

Here is a jubilant song in praise of God's fatherly love, one of the finest in the Psalter. "Forget not all his benefits," (v.2) the psalmist counsels, and then enumerates a number of those benefits.

Hosea 2:14-23

Israel, because of her apostasy, is considered an unfaithful wife whom God is willing to take back and to whom he will become re-betrothed. The warmth of divine compassion is one of the benefits from the Lord of which we ought to be continually mindful. (Note: Jezreel - "God sows" - was the name given Israel in her apostasy; once a name of judgment, now it is a name of promise. Read "God sows" and the meaning is clear without explanation.)

II Corinthians 3: [4-11] 17-4:2

The risen Lord who first appeared to the apostle on the Damascus road is his inspiration and the motivating force. The presence of this risen Lord is the Holy Spirit (3:18), and this Spirit gives life. The conviction of this sufficiency carries with it a great sense of freedom. In his way Paul is saying, "Know the truth and the truth will make you free" (Jn. 8:32).

Mark 2:18-22

Being with Jesus turned his disciples' lives around. Their resulting behavior, as well as his words, created the opposition to Jesus which ultimately brought him to the cross. Jesus still turns lives around. When we are alive to his presence, we are alive to his benefits.

Proper 4 (Closest to June 1)

B

Theme: God's Commandments

Psalm 81 [at the Eucharist: vss. 1-10]

This was probably a New Year's festival hymn, and it makes clear that the reason God gave Israel the Commandments was that he desires to save (vss.7, 13).

Deuteronomy 5:6-21

The Ten Commandments have always been considered a succinct statement of how God expects man to behave in relation to God and in relation to his fellows.

(Lead in: *"Moses summoned all Israel and said to them, 'Hear, O Israel, the statutes and ordinances of the Lord our God: I am the Lord. . . .' ")*

II Corinthians 4:5-12

"The light of the knowledge of the glory of God" (and also of his will for us) is found in Jesus Christ. It is he who warms our hearts and transforms our lives so that we are willing to undergo anything in order that "the life of Jesus may be manifested in our bodies" (v.10).

Mark 2:23-28

Unquestionably, the Ten Commandments are God's will for his people. But by Jesus' day religious leaders had come to make a fetish of minutiae, so that the law had become a vehicle of pride, arrogance, and separation. Jesus attacks this corruption. He is the Savior from all that divides and degrades, even holy things. Here lies the root of the opposition which ultimately brought him to the cross (3:6).

(Lead in: *"On one sabbath Jesus was going. . . . "*

Proper 5 (Closest to June 8)

B

Theme: Man's sin and God's grace

Psalm 130

This has been the favorite psalm of many through the ages, including Martin Luther. It is the confession of a Godfearing man who moves from deep anguish brought on by his sin, to a profound conviction of divine grace and forgiveness.

Genesis 3: [1-7] 8-21

This O.T. myth (i.e., eternal truth conveyed in a story) succinctly explains the nature of sin. Sin is the temptation to become God's rival (v.5), not just his child. The human temptation from the beginning has been to blame someone else for one's transgressions. God's grace is also apparent here. The Lord does not turn his back on Adam and Eve; even though he punishes them he also takes care of them.

II Corinthians 4:13-18
The apostle makes clear that to believe in the Lord's resurrection is the source of comfort and sustaining power, especially for those who are victims of illness or affliction. "He who raised up Jesus the Lord will. . . bring us. . . into his presence. . . so we do not lose heart" (vss.14, 16). In the hard school of suffering, many, like Paul, have learned that God is gracious.

Mark 3:20-35
Sin is the work of the devil, who has sought to be God's rival from the beginning and would transform us into his likeness. Jesus said that the sin against the Holy Spirit was our failure to recognize that Satanic motivation in our own behavior. If one cannot distinguish between the Spirit of God and the spirit of evil, one is truly beyond help.

(Lead in: *"The crowd came together again so that Jesus and his disciples could not. . . ."*)

Proper 6 (Closest to June 15)

B

Theme: The judgment of God/Grow in the Lord.

Psalm 92 [at the Eucharist: vss.1-4, 11-14]
This psalm reflects the meaning of Jesus' parable of growth from seed to harvest. "The wicked grow like weeds" (v.6), and "the righteous shall flourish like a palm tree" (v.11). At the harvest, what one has done will be important.

Ezekiel 31:1-6, 10-14
Among the prophet's oracles against the nations is this pronouncement of doom on Egypt. The glory and vaunted pride of Egypt will be brought low by Nebuchadnezzar. God is the judge of the nations and the ruler of history; both men and nations should live accordingly.

II Corinthians 5:1-10
In writing about the nature of the apostolic ministry, Paul speaks of his hope of an eternal home. His conclusion is that the important thing is to be ready always for judgment, so that at all times we "make it our aim to please him" (v.9).

Mark 4:26-34

Among Jesus' parables are those which make clear that our goal is to grow into the kind of persons whose lives are pleasing to God. When the harvest comes, each will receive "good or evil, according to what he has done in the body" (II Cor.5:10).

Proper 7 (Closest to June 22)

B

Theme: Lord of the storms of nature and of men

Psalm 107:1-32 [at the Eucharist: vss. 1-3, 23-32]

This psalm of thanksgiving is a series of stanzas each with a twofold refrain thanking God for deliverance from being lost in a desert, from prison, from sickness, and from a storm at sea. The last-named makes us think of the experience of the disciples in the boat with Jesus. "He stilled the storm. . . . Then they were glad. . . . Let us then give thanks to the Lord. . . ." (vss. 28-30).

Job 38:1-11, 16-18

In the course of this drama, after Job's friends have ceased giving him advice and Job has spun out the extent of his anguish of soul and frustration, God finally speaks. In the lofty majesty of the opening stanzas of the Lord's reply we catch an awesome glimpse of the Creator almost in the act of creating the seas.

II Corinthians 5:14-21

Reconciliation is the key to an understanding of the Christian faith. What Christ did was done so that we might be reconciled to God, and in our turn we respond by seeking to be the agents of reconciliation among our fellows.

Mark 4:35-41; [5:1-20]

The power of the God who is Creator of the seas and Lord of the storms in the O.T. is also seen in Jesus. No wonder his disciples in the boat asked one another in awe, "Who then is this?" Jesus' command, "Peace, be still," has authority beyond the world of nature. He is Lord also over the evil forces which rend people's lives. To the man in the tombs possessed by an evil spirit he also said, "Peace, be still."

(Lead in: *"On that day, when evening had come, Jesus said to his disciples. . . ."*)

Proper 8 (Closest to June 29)

B

Theme: Be generous to the poor/The giver of life

Psalm 112

In the psalmist's description of "the man who fears the Lord" he says that he is "generous in lending" and gives "freely to the poor" (vss.5, 9)

Deuteronomy 15:7-11

In his discussion of the year of release, Moses enunciates and explains the ancient law regarding treatment of the poor.

II Corinthians 8:1-9, 13-15

Chapters 8 and 9 are a unit describing a collection made for needy Christians in Jerusalem. A sense of stewardship—giving to relieve the needs of others—is one of the ways in which the Christian lives a life acceptable to God.

Mark 5:22-24, 35b-43

The serial reading of Mark's Gospel continues with the account of the raising of the daughter of Jairus, the ruler of the synagogue. The appeal comes to Jesus when the child is *in extremis*, beyond human help. The point is that Jairus believes Jesus has supernatural power and can bestow healing and life. (One literal meaning of the word "salvation" is "to save alive.")

(Lead in: begin with v.21.)

Proper 9 (Closest to July 6)

B

Theme: God's Spokesmen

Psalm 123

In this brief, unpretentious prayer the suffering of the nation is lifted up to God with moving tenderness. In the context of today's Scripture, it might be thought of as the prayer of one of God's spokesmen: "Have mercy upon us. . . for we have had more than enough of contempt" (v.4).

Ezekiel 2:1-7

This is the account of Ezekiel's call to be God's spokesman (what "prophet" literally means). He is warned that people may not listen to him, but this lack of reception is not to deter him.

II Corinthians 12:2-10

Here is an autobiographical glimpse into the life of Paul. He was one of God's spokesmen—"a man in Christ" (v.2). Not being listened to was only a part of his suffering. His attitude toward both his physical affliction and the sufferings inflicted by others sets a Christian standard which gives us much to think about.

Mark 6:1-6
The Israelites had turned a deaf ear to the prophets of old; now their descendants would not listen to Jesus. Notice that there is a direct relation between people's capacity to believe and the possibility of God's power being evident in their midst.

Proper 10 (Closest to July 13)

B

Theme: The Lord's spokesmen

Psalm 85 [at the Eucharist: vss. 7-13]
This magnificent psalm is in two parts. The congregation rehearses God's mighty acts in the past (vs. 1-3); then follows a deeply moving supplication because of present affliction (vs, 4-7). Now a prophet rises to his feet and recounts the vision of hope and comfort which has just come to him (vs. 8-13).

Amos 7:7-15
Amos had a vision of a divine plumb line of justice in the midst of the people of Israel, which found them failing to measure up. Because of his message, Amos was unpopular; however, he could not but obey the divine compulsion to be the Lord's spokesman.
(Lead in: *"Thus the Lord God showed me. . . ."*)

Ephesians 1:1-14
This epistle, which we shall hear read serially for the next eight weeks, opens with an act of thanksgiving, which is essentially an outline of the writer's Christian belief. Every phrase here deserves careful consideration.

Mark 6:7-13
Midway in his ministry, Jesus sends out the Twelve to proclaim the kingdom and prepare people to receive him. Jesus warns that being his spokesmen will not always be easy or popular.
(Lead in: *"Jesus called to him. . . ."*)

Proper 11 (Closest to July 20)

B

Theme: Christ is our peace.

Psalm 22:22-30

This second half of a psalm which we associate with Jesus' passion is a psalm of thanksgiving. Read over against the other appointed Scripture for this day we especially hear: "to him alone all. . . bow down in worship" and "they shall. . . make known. . . the saving deeds that he has done" (vss.28, 30).

Isaiah 57:14-21

In the beautiful poetry of Second Isaiah, we find these stanzas about God abiding with his people. In part that presence is judgment, but people also experience healing and comfort and peace.

Ephesians 2:11-22

In the doctrinal part of this epistle, the author explains the spiritual unity of mankind in the Church. The healing and peace for which people yearn comes true in Jesus Christ. Because he dwells in our midst, "the dividing wall of hostility" crumbles.

Mark 6:30-44

Jesus' feeding of the Five Thousand is interwoven in our thinking with the Last Supper, which our Lord identifies as the foretaste of the messianic banquet (14:25). The messianic banquet is a symbol of brotherhood. One does not break bread with strangers or enemies.

Proper 12 (Closest to July 27)

B

Theme: The spirit that molds our lives/Lord over nature and the human heart

Psalm 114

This festival hymn praises God for the wonders he wrought in the time of Moses. God was Lord of the waters—the Red Sea and the River Jordan (v.3)—in Israel's past.

II Kings 2:1-15

This is the end of the Elijah saga: his translation into heaven and the commissioning of Elisha as his successor. History remembers these two as God-fearing men, and all the stories about them are intended to convey that fact.

Ephesians 4:1-7, 11-16

This is the beginning of the ethical half of Ephesians. Elisha received something of the spirit of Elijah, the godly man whom he succeeded (II Kings 2:15). The N.T. Christians also received something of the Spirit of their Lord, the God-man. His Spirit knit them together and created a body (the Church) which matures as it moves toward "the measure of the stature of the fulness of Christ" (v.13).

Mark 6:45-52

This little incident occurred immediately after the feeding of the five thousand. In the disciples' remembrance of Jesus, they recognized that he was Lord over the physical world as well as the spiritual. His presence restored calm to their storm-tossed outer world as well as bringing peace to their troubled hearts.

Proper 13 (Closest to August 3)

B

Theme: The bread of life

Psalm 78:1-25 [at the Eucharist: vss.14-20, 23-25]

Israel's faith was historical, not philosophical. It was grounded in the way God had dealt with their ancestors. Other psalms recount this history (e.g. Pss.105, 106), but in this psalm the poet reflects on "that which we have heard and known" (v.3). Verses 14 through 25 deal in part with the manna from heaven in the wilderness.

Exodus 16:2-4, 9-15

This is the account of how God fed the Israelites with manna in the wilderness. Christian liturgy is deeply rooted in this O.T. idea of bread from heaven with which God fed his people.

Ephesians 4:17-25

The Sunday-by-Sunday serial reading of this epistle brings us today to a central section of the ethical part of this book. It is sermonic and was probably originally read in church.

John 6:24-35

Following the account of the feeding of the five thousand, John's Gospel has an extended discourse in its meaning. This portion of that discourse looks back to the manna from heaven in the wilderness and looks forward to the significance of the Last Supper.

Proper 14 (Closest to August 10)

B

Theme: The bread which came down from heaven

Psalm 34 [at the Eucharist: vss.1-8]

This thanksgiving has from early times been associated with the Lord's

Supper because of the words "Taste and see that the Lord is good" (v.8). It turns our minds both to the manna from heaven and "the bread which comes down from heaven. . . for the life of the world" (Jn. 6:50-51).

Deuteronomy 8:1-10
Moses reminds the Israelites of God's watchful providence during their forty years in the wilderness and exhorts them to keep God's commandments in the days ahead when they enter the Promised Land.
(Lead in: *"Moses said, 'All the commandments. . . .' "*)

Ephesians 4: [25-29] 30-5:2
Because a Christian is a believer in the risen Christ, his character and his conduct are transformed. Here the author is spelling out what in another place is called being "a new creation" (II Cor. 5:17).

John 6: 37-51
The discourse in this chapter on the significance of the feeding of the five thousand is one of the N.T.'s fullest commentaries on the Eucharist. (Another is in I Corinthians 11.)
(Lead in: *"Jesus said, 'All that the Father. . . .'"*)

Proper 15 (Closest to August 17)

B

Theme: The gifts of God

Psalm 147
This psalm has two interlocking themes: the power of God and his compassionate grace as manifested in creation and election. It enumerates the gifts with which God has expressed his deep concern for those whom he created and has chosen for his own.

Alternate psalm at the Eucharist: Psalm 34:9-14
"Those who fear him lack nothing" (v.9). Resolute trust opens one's eyes to the gifts of God.

Proverbs 9:1-6
God's gift of wisdom is here pictured as a busy housewife. The "simple" person referred to is one open to any influence. The bread and wine Madam Wisdom offers is the gift of a long, prosperous, and happy life, nothing more.

Ephesians 5:15-20
This passage sums up the writer's exhortation to have done with pagan ways (4:17-5:20). He uses "wise" in the sense of that practical wisdom that makes conduct consistent with faith.

John 6:53-59

Here is the conclusion of the Lord's discourse on the inner meaning of the Eucharist (6:27-59). This passage stands in stark contrast to that from Proverbs. Both use (or imply) the words bread, wine, and life, but oh, what a difference: the bread of earth and the bread of heaven, a happy and prosperous life in this world and eternal life.

Proper 16 (Closest to August 24)

B

Theme: Decision: whom will you serve?

Psalm 16 [at the Eucharist: vss. 1-8]

In this ancient affirmation of trust, the psalmist says, "You are my Lord, my good above all other" (v.1).

Alternate psalm at the Eucharist: Psalm 34:15-22

The psalmist's answer to "Whom will you serve?" is to vest his faith in the God who sustains and defends him.

Joshua 24:1-2a, 14-25

Joshua was Moses' successor, who led the Israelites into the Promised Land. Now at the end of his days, he urges Israel to renew its covenant with the God who delivered them from Egypt and brought them into the land they now inhabit. He commands them to choose between the God of their fathers and the gods of the peoples in whose land they now dwell, and he leaves no doubt as to where his loyalty lies.

Ephesians 5:21-33

In the ethical section of this epistle, the writer uses the relationship of Christ and his Church as a model for husband-wife relations.

John 6:60-69

When Jesus speaks of himself as "the bread which came down from heaven" and adds that "he who eats this bread will live for ever" (v.58), he utters a "hard saying" which some cannot believe. In effect Jesus says to his disciples, as Joshua said to the Israelites, "Choose you this day whom you will serve." Peter, speaking for his brethren vested his confidence in the Lord.

(Lead in: Add vss. 57-59 to the reading and begin, *"Jesus said, 'As the living Father sent me. . .'"*)

Proper 17 (Closest to August 31)

B

Theme: God's Law—straightforward or twisted

Psalm 15

Here is a picture of a person of "blameless life." He seeks to do what is right in God's sight, and there is no ulterior motive in his behavior, no guile.

Deuteronomy 4:1-9

Moses exhorts the Israelites to keep the law, pointing out the privileges which are theirs because of God's nearness and concern for them. He warns against "adding to the word," which by the time of Jesus had become not only a corruption of the law but also of those who were its custodians.

(Lead in: *"Moses said, 'Now, O Israel, give heed. . . .' "*]

Ephesians 6:10-20

The Christian warrior is exhorted to wear the same spiritual armor in which God is clothed when he goes forth to overthrow his enemies (Isa. 59:17). This is the way in which to contend successfully against the rulers of darkness and the spiritual hosts of wickedness.

Mark 7:1-8, 14-15, 21-23

Judaism in Jesus' day was well-nigh smothered by oral tradition which overlay the commandments. The source of unrighteousness is not in violation of ritual regulations but in succumbing to the rulers of darkness which struggle for possession of our inmost being.

(Lead in: *"Now when the Pharisees gathered together to Jesus. . . .").*

Proper 18 (Closest to September 7)

B

Theme: Healing and deliverance come from God.

Psalm 146 [at the Eucharist: vss. 4-9]

The psalmist sings of his trust in God. One of the reasons for his exuberant praise is the Lord's healing goodness: he "opens the eyes of the blind" (v.6).

Isaiah 35:4-7a

To the Babylonian exiles, the prophet sings of God's saving power. The glory of the Lord will be a transformed world in which the blind see, the deaf hear, and the dumb speak.

(Later in the poem he also foresees the exiles' return to Zion, v.10.)

James 1: 17-27

Here is the first of a series of four readings from this little, practical book on Christian behavior which appeared during the latter part of the first century. The writer's primary concern is with what a Christian does rather than what he believes.

Mark 7:31-37

Mark makes it clear that Jesus' ministry is the messianic fulfillment of O.T. prophecy. Behind this account quite obviously lies Isaiah 35. The people's comment, "He has done all things well," literally means, "How exactly he fulfills the prophecies!"

(Lead in: *"When Jesus returned from. . . ."*)

Proper 19 (Closest to September 14)

B

Theme: The suffering servant of the Lord/Deliverance by the power of God

Psalm 116 [at the Eucharist: vss. 1-8)

This is a psalm of thanksgiving for deliverance. We sense that there has been mortal terror and deep anguish. The poet has experienced bitterness and despair. Now he has reached the quiet happiness of a heart sheltered in the love of God.

Isaiah 50:4-9

This is the second of four "servant poems" in Second Isaiah. The writer may have been thinking of an individual or of the nation as a whole or of the coming Messiah, but N.T. writers saw in his words a description of the passion of our Lord.

James 2:1-5, 8-10, 14-18

The writer deals with behavior in the church in terms of "You shall love your neighbor as yourself." In vss. 14-18 we have a major theme of this epistle. The writer's views on faith and works seem to contradict those of Paul (Rom. 3:28). Actually, he is contradicting a distortion of Paul's thesis which he considered blasphemy.

Mark 8:27-38

At the critical midway point of his ministry, Jesus asks the disciples about people's opinion of him—others, and their own. When Peter, always the spokesman of the Twelve, answered, "You are the Christ," Jesus began to explain what kind of Messiah he was to be. Peter objected and Jesus rebuked him. Jesus was thinking of his vocation as the "suffering servant" poems had described it. That possibility had never crossed the minds of his followers.

Alternate Gospel: Mark 9:14-29

Isaiah's description of the suffering servant couples the suffering he is willing to endure with the power "to sustain with a word him that is weary" (50:4). The father of the convulsed child experienced this power.

(Lead in: *"When Jesus and his companions came to the other disciples. . . ."*)

Proper 20 (Closest to September 21)

B

Theme: The price of righteousness

Psalm 54

The psalmist is persecuted and his life threatened by violent and overbearing enemies. We are likely to identify him with our Lord as he foresaw his passion and death.

Wisdom 1:16-2:1 [6-11] 12-22

The ungodly man finds the very presence of the righteous person a judgment on his thoughts and ways. The Christian cannot hear these words without associating them with the religious leaders' attitude toward Jesus.

James 3:16-4:6

James is an earnest, common-sense moralist who is wholly concerned with everyday conduct. This passage is a clear example of why that is the case.

Mark 9:30-37

This is our Lord's second prediction that he will suffer and die (see 8:31f). The freely accepted suffering which awaits Jesus is not an isolated, accidental occurrence, but exemplifies a law of the kingdom which applies equally to all who would enter its life. The author of the Book of Wisdom was aware of this truth.

Proper 21 (Closest to September 28)

Theme: Rejoice that the Spirit blows where it wills.

B

Psalm 19 [at the Eucharist: vss. 7-14]

Here are two dissimilar poems: a nature poem (vss. 1-6) and one exalting the Mosaic Law (vss. 7-14). The reason for reading it on this day lies in the reference to presumptuous sins (v. 13), of which, as we see, both Moses' and Jesus' followers were guilty.

Numbers 11:4-6, 10-16, 24-29
In this wilderness encounter, there is some insight into the O.T. thinking about the Spirit of God. No one doubted that God's Spirit rested on Moses. But Joshua was more concerned for his master's honor and privilege than for the ways of God and the good of the whole people. Here also is the early O.T. conviction that the Spirit "blows where it will" (Jn. 3:8).

James 4:7-12 [13-5:6]
This latter part of James' epistle contains an almost random list of injunctions on Christian behavior.

Mark 9:38-43, 45, 47-48
It is a temptation of loyal followers to be jealous for their leader's reputation and to want to put down any potential rivals. Jesus' disciples showed this tendency, not realizing that the Spirit of God can work in many ways through diverse people. A number of Jesus' sayings have unaccountably been gathered up in this chapter.
(Lead in: *"John said to Jesus, 'Teacher. . . .' "*)

Proper 22 (Closest to October 5)

B

Theme: Man and woman in God's creative plan

Psalm 8
This is a hymn in praise of the Creator, and mankind is a wonderful part of that creation.

Alternate psalm: Psalm 128
Here is a pilgrim's song. Domestic blessings were considered the result of a person's godliness.

Genesis 2:18-24
In the second creation story (2:4-24) we have this account of the creation of woman. The point is that man and woman are a unit; they belong together. "It is not good that man should be alone" (v.18).

Hebrews 2: [1-8] 9-18
In chapter one the author has told us who Jesus Christ is. In this chapter he gives a preview of Jesus' work of salvation.

Mark 10:2-9

In the time of Jesus the Genesis story of the creation of man and woman was being used in support of monogamy. Jesus appears to see it as prohibiting divorce. There is scholarly disagreement as to the meaning of the words, "Those whom God has joined together. . ." (v.9). Do they mean, "Let not man (any human authority) lightly separate," or "Let not man separate for any reason of his own"? Certainly monogamous marriage is intended to be permanent. Exceptions cannot be proven or disproven from this passage.

Proper 23 (Closest to October 12)

B

Theme: The way that leads to life

Psalm 90 [at the Eucharist: vss. 1-8, 12]

An old man looks at life in an earnest, comprehensive way. He sees it in eternal perspective and prays that this will be true for all (v.12).

Amos 5:6-7, 10-15

These verses give us the kernel of the prophet's message. He denounces evil and repeatedly urges that his hearers seek good and not evil "that you may live" (v. 14). He also holds out the possibility that the just God will be gracious to those who turn from evil. The theme of his book is summed up in v.15.

Hebrews 3:1-6

The major thrust of this book is that Jesus Christ is the final and perfect revelation of God. The author first argued that he is superior to angels (chaps 1-2). Now he makes clear that Jesus Christ is superior to Moses.

Mark 10:12-27 [28-31]

The man who comes to Jesus with his question about what to do to inherit eternal life might be answered, "There is more to man's relationship with God than negative blamelessness with respect to the law" (Nineham: *Mark*.) One must also put one's whole trust in God as the sole source of security and well-being. Moreover, the possession of wealth can be an insuperable barrier.

Proper 24 (Closest to October 19)

B

Theme: By his stripes we are healed.

Psalm 91 [at the Eucharist: vss. 9-16)

This is an impressive testimony to the strength which springs from profound trust in God. The opening part promises divine protection to the person of deep trust (vss. 1-13). In verses 14-16, God addresses that individual and the promise is confirmed. These latter verses suggest the reassurance which was the Lord's strength in his passion

Isaiah 53:4-12

This is part of the most famous of the servant poems. Whether the poet was describing the vicarious suffering of an individual, such as Jeremiah, or of the whole nation of Israel, or was looking into the future, we do not know. The early Christians saw in it a description of the Lord's passion, and it has so colored the Gospel accounts that we cannot think of these words in any other connection.

Hebrews 4:12-16

This portion of the Sunday-by-Sunday serial reading of this epistle brackets two emphases. After a discussion of the incisive nature of the word of God, there is the beginning of a section on Christ as the heavenly high priest, an idea which we usually associate with the Lord's ascension.

Mark 10:35-45

Interwoven with Jesus' prediction of his passion is the story of the disciples' selfish request. "The cup that I drink" and "the baptism with which I am baptized" both refer to his passion, which he foresees will be giving his "life as a ransom for many."

Proper 25 (Closest to October 26)

B

Theme: The blind seek and find salvation.

Psalm 13

This is the simple lament of a sick person searching for the light of faith in the midst of discouraging circumstances: "How long will you forget me. . . ? . . .give light to my eyes. . .I put my trust in your mercy. . .your saving help."

Isaiah 59: [1-4] 9-19

The fact that salvation is far off (v.11) does not mean that the Lord does not hear or cannot save; rather it is because the people's sins separate them from God (vss. 1-2). So an impenitent people grope like the blind. But when the community turns from lament to confession, God—the Redeemer—comes.

Hebrews 5:12-6:1, 9-12

The Sunday-by-Sunday serial reading of this epistle continues. After explaining the role of Jesus Christ as the heavenly high priest, the writer addresses his readers, who are expected to understand and teach this truth. He is at first stern, then encouraging.

Mark 10:46-52

The early Church saw in the healing of the blind man a universal symbol. His blind groping, his call for help and his coming to Jesus, and the fact that he received healing (salvation) following his cry for mercy, made him the prototype of every man.

(Lead in: *"Jesus and his disciples came. . . ."*)

Proper 26 (Closest to November 2)

B

Theme: The law of the Lord

Psalm 119:1-16 [at the Eucharist: vss. 1-8)

These are the first two stanzas of a long, stylized poem in praise of God's law.

Deuteronomy 6:1-9

The Ten Commandments are in the previous chapter. Here Moses emphasizes the importance of observing them. This passage includes the *Shema* (vss. 4-5), which we know as our Lord's first and great commandment. Every Jew was expected to recite it every day.

(Lead in: *"Moses said, 'Now this is. . .' "*)

Hebrews 7:23-28

In this chapter the author shows the superiority of Jesus' heavenly priesthood to the Levitical priesthood of the O.T.

Mark 12:28-34

The scribes debated among themselves as to which was the most important commandment, meaning not just the Ten Commandments but also the 700-odd rabbinical elaborations which had by Jesus' time come to be associated with the Decalogue. In his reply, Jesus (perhaps for the first time) associated the neighbor commandment (Lev. 19:18) with the *Shema* (Deut. 6:4-5).

(Lead in: *"One of the scribes came up and heard Jesus and the Sadducees disputing. . . ."*)

Proper 27 (Closest to November 9)

Theme: Complete trust in God

Psalm 146 [at the Eucharist: vss. 4-9]
This simple hymn of trust in God exudes joyful faith partly because the psalmist has unwavering belief that God will provide "food to the hungry" and will sustain the fatherless and widow (vss. 5, 7).

I Kings 17:8-16
Elijah the prophet is first seen when he tells King Ahab of Israel that there will be a severe drought because of the king's misdoings (17:1). As a result of this, the prophet had to flee from the king's wrath. What he asks of the widow at Zarephath is to use her last supplies and cook him something to eat, telling her that God will take care of her and her son. The miracle performed by this man of God has a counterpart in the faith of the widow.
(Lead in: *"Then the word of the Lord came to Elijah. . . ."*)

Hebrews 9:24-28
In explaining the ministry of Jesus as a high priest, the author makes clear the finality of redemption brought about by Christ's death, in contrast to the temporary benefits of the sacrifices offered by the high priest in the temple.

Mark 12:38-44
Here is a beautiful vignette in which Jesus comments on the offering of a poor widow whom he observes putting her pittance into the temple treasury. Like the widow of Zarephath (I Kings 17:18) she gives all that she has to God and trusts in his merciful care.
(Lead in: *"In his teaching Jesus said. . . ."*)

Proper 28 (Closest to November 16)

Theme: The day of judgment

Psalm 16 [at the Eucharist: vss. 5-11]
This is the prayer of one who may be facing death. In any case, his calm and faithful attitude enables him to see beyond the grave. For such a one the day of judgment has lost its fearfulness.

Daniel 12:1-4a [5-13]
The Book of Daniel closes with this vision of the last days. Here is both the end of tribulation and resurrection. "Those who sleep in the dust of the

earth shall awaken, some to everlasting life, some to contempt" (v.2). The author goes on to sum up all he has been saying about the last days: "Some shall purify themselves. . . but the wicked shall do wickedly" (v.10).

(Lead in: *"The Lord spoke to Daniel, saying. . . ."*)

Hebrews 10:31-39

The latter part of this chapter (10:19ff.) asserts that our Christian commitment is not to be taken lightly, for failure means a fearful judgment. In this reading the author is dealing principally with judgment. On the one hand, "it is a fearful thing to fall into the hands of the living God" (v. 31). On the other, "we are not of those who shrink back. . .but of those who have faith and keep their souls" (v.39).

Mark 13:14-23

Jesus' apocalyptic prediction probably reached its present literary form at a time when the Church's thinking was colored by a catastrophic historical event—the fall of Jerusalem. The point is that when the day of judgment is at hand, all the foundations of life will be shaken, and only those who place their faith in a merciful God will be saved.

(Lead in: *"Jesus said, 'But when you see. . . .' "*)

Last Proper (29) (Closest to November 23)

B

Theme: Stand in awe of the King of kings.

Psalm 93

The psalmist sings the praise of the Lord as King. The heavenly enthronement here is of a piece with the majesty and overarching rule of God about which we hear in the other readings on this day.

Daniel 7:9-14

Here is part of a vision of the court of heaven. "One like a son of man" is presented before "the Ancient of Days" and is given "everlasting dominion" over nations and peoples. Phrases from this passage probably lie behind the language of the Lord's Prayer: "hallowed be thy name," "thine is the kingdom," and the like.

Revelation 1:1-8

The opening part of this book is written like a series of letters. In John's description of the risen Christ as "ruler of the kings of the earth" and of the Father's eternal dominion we catch something of the awesomeness of his vision.

John 18:33-37

In the midst of the Lord's passion, he and Pilate the Roman governor come face to face. Jesus sets his kingship in the eternal realm and thus raises his passion to the level of eternal significance.

Alternate Gospel: Mark 11:1-11

In the course of Jesus' triumphal entry into Jerusalem, the shouts of the crowd ring truer than they know. He was coming in the name of the "Ancient of Days" (Dan. 7:13) and his kingdom had heavenly significance, as Daniel and the author of Revelation foresaw.

Lead in: *"When Jesus and his disciples drew. . . ."*)

The Sunday Lectionary

Year C

First Sunday of Advent

Theme: Prepare to meet the eternal Judge.

Psalm 50 [at the Eucharist: vss. 1-6]
    This dramatic psalm is a liturgy in which God, the righteous Judge, appears (vss. 1, 6-7) and passes judgment on both the excessive emphasis on cultic practices by the faithful (vss. 7-15) and the lax observance of the commandments by the wicked (vss. 16-21).

Zechariah 14:4-9
    Anonymous prophecies are attached to the end of this little book (Zech. 9-14). This passage, which is part of a prophecy about the last days, captures the flavor of the Advent season: "The Lord your God will come, and . . . will become king over all the earth" (vss. 5, 9).
    (Lead in: *"On the day of battle the Lord's feet shall. . . ."*)

I Thessalonians 3:9-13
    The two letters to the church in Thessalonica are the earliest parts of the N.T., written about 50 A.D. This warm passage closes with a prayer that the lives of the Thessalonian Christians may be blameless in the day of the return of the Lord Jesus. The return of the crucified and risen Christ is a dominant Advent theme.

Luke 21:25-31
    A central conviction of first-century Christians was that Christ would shortly return in glory as Judge. Chapter 21 of Luke is devoted to evidences of that coming great day. It is writ deep in the creeds, but we mistakenly tend to shrug off the subject as unimportant because it is so prominent an emphasis among the fringe sects of Christendom.
    (Lead in: *"Jesus said, 'There will be signs. . . . ' "*)

Second Sunday of Advent

Theme: The great day of the coming of Jesus Christ is imminent.

Psalm 126
    Of the "great things" (vss. 3-4) God has done for us, sending his Son as the Savior of the world heads the list.

Baruch 5:1-9
    The tenor of this poetry is reminiscent of Isaiah 40-55. The same consolation and promise are here that were addressed to the exiles in

Babylon shortly before they returned to their own land. The spirit is also that of Advent, foretelling the coming of "the light of his glory with mercy and righteousness" (v.9).

Philippians 1:1-11

Paul's opening words to the members of the church at Philippi are almost a prayer. The Advent flavor of this passage comes out in the words, "I am sure that he who began a good work in you will bring it to completion at the day of Jesus Christ" (v.6).

Luke 3:1-6

Luke was a sober historian. With these words he carefully dates his account of when the word of the Lord came to John the Baptist, the Advent figure who heralded Jesus' coming.

Third Sunday of Advent

C

Theme: Prepare for the coming of the Lord.

Psalm 85 [at the Eucharist: vss. 7-13]

This psalm of comfort and hope contains both the yearning for the salvation of the Lord (v.7). and the promise that that divine blessing will shortly come to God's people (v.9). It echoes the notes of yearning and expectancy which run through the Advent season.

Alternate to the psalm: Canticle 9, Ecce, Deus [Isaiah 12:2-6]

This Morning Prayer canticle has an appropriate Advent flavor in speaking of the Lord as Savior and of the coming day of salvation, when "the great one (is) in the midst of you."

Zephaniah 3:14-20

The prophet's words heard at this time of year cannot but have Christmas overtones. "The Lord is in your midst; you shall fear evil no more" (v.15) is of a piece with the angel's announcement to the shepherds: "Fear not, for unto you is born. . . a Savior" (Lk. 2:10-11).

Philippians 4:4-7 [8-9]

Paul is writing from a Roman prison shortly before his death. "The Lord is at hand" has eternal significance for him, but also for us. Christmas will celebrate the Lord's final coming as our Judge along with recalling his first coming long ago. Our preparation for his coming is both internal and external. The "peace which passes all understanding" will be ours only if we have striven to live lives worthy of him.

Luke 3:7-18

This is the fullest account of the impact of John the Baptist's ministry on the people of his day. He created a climate of national repentance. He prepared people for the coming of God's Messiah.

(Lead in: *"John the baptizer said to the multitudes. . . . "*)

Fourth Sunday of Advent

C

Theme: Come, Lord Jesus.

Psalm 80 [at the Eucharist: vss. 1-7]

This psalm was a community lament probably at the time of an enemy invasion. When we hear these words, our Christmas-oriented thoughts find their appropriateness in their yearning for the coming of the Lord who has the power to save.

Micah 5:2-4

This part of one of the prophet's visions of a glorious future is for us a Christmas prediction. It is this prophecy which is quoted in the story of the Wise Men coming to worship the Christ Child (Matt. 2:5-6). The poem sings of God's universal rule of justice and peace.

Hebrews 10:5-10

The writer makes it clear that a new order of things begins with the coming of Jesus Christ.

(Lead in: *"When Christ came into the world. . . "*)

Luke 1:39-49 (50-56)

Here is the setting in which the *Magnificat,* one of the Bible's most lovely hymns, occurs. Hearing it is obviously appropriate on the eve of Christmas.

Christmas Day, First Proper

C

Theme: Christ the Savior is born.

Psalm 96 [at the Eucharist: vss. 1-4, 11-12]

For the Christian, almost every verse of this psalm has to do with the Savior's birth.

Isaiah 9:2-4, 6-7

The prophet wrote this poem about the Messiah who was to come. It is impossible to read it without seeing in it a full-blown description of our Lord and his mission.

Titus 2:11-14

This epistle, written perhaps one hundred years after the crucifixion - resurrection, contains practical advice to leaders of the early Church. This section is particularly appropriate on Christmas Day.

Luke 2:1-14 [15-20]

This wonderful prose-poetry gives us an unforgettable picture of the nativity. The angel's announcement is for all time the classic statement of the Good News.

Christmas Day, Second Proper

C

Theme: Christ the Lord has come.

Psalm 97 [at the Eucharist: vss. 1-2, 8-12)

The special character of this psalm "allows an insight into the depth and comprehension of the O.T. idea of the kingdom of God" (Weiser). This is appropriate at the celebration of the birth of him who ushered in that kingdom.

Isaiah 62:6-7, 10-12

Chapter 62 describes in a poem the people of God, the messianic people. In the first of these two stanzas the people are in tiptoe expectancy. The second describes that people when the Messiah (Greek, Christ) has come. Here is the source of our Christmas joy.

Titus 3:4-7

This advice to early Christian leaders becomes an appropriate sermonette when we hear it on this day.

Luke 2: [1-14] 15-20

Our whole Biblical memory of Christmas centers in the angelic announcement to the shepherds and their visit to the manger babe.

Christmas Day, Third Proper

Theme: The Word has become flesh and dwells among us.

Psalm 98 [at the Eucharist: vss. 1-6]

The coming of Jesus Christ gives the "new song" of the psalmist deeper significance than he dreamed of. All creation is exhorted (vss. 7-9), along with God's people, to sing of the marvelous things God has done (v.1).

Isaiah 52:7-10
These glorious verses are from a poem which might be entitled "The Lord Has Become King" (51:17-52:12). Here the arrival of the bearer of good news is described in unforgettable words.

Hebrews 1:1-12
This first chapter of Hebrews describes the incarnation of God's Son in terms of its eternal significance.

John 1:1-14
The Fourth Gospel describes the coming of God's Son from the point of view of God's eternal purpose and of man's response. The meaning of "Word" is pivotal. It embraces God's creative power, his purpose, his wisdom and his providence.

First Sunday after Christmas

C

Theme: God's grace is manifested in Jesus Christ.

Psalm 147 [at the Eucharist: vss. 12-21]
This psalm contains the essence of Hebrew worship. God is praised because of his power and because of "his compassionate grace as manifested in creation and election" (Weiser). With the coming of Jesus Christ, God's grace has been set in a higher key.

Isaiah 61:10-62:3
In some of the most stirring poetry of the Bible an ancient seer sings of the glad tidings of salvation to Zion. Heard on this day these words become part of the profound joy of this feast of Christ's nativity.

Galatians 3:23-25; 4:4-7
With the coming of Christ, man's relation to God has changed, radically, from legalism to faith. Paul explains that the discipline of trying to keep the law was the training that prepares us for faith in Christ's merciful power. The emphasis has changed from seeking to gain God's favor by the good works we do to putting our faith in his love for us. It is the difference between a slave and an adopted son.

John 1:1-18
The Prologue of John's Gospel also makes clear the point of the Galatians passage above. "The law was given through Moses; grace and

truth came through Jesus Christ" (v.17). "Grace" here means undeserved, unexpected kindness and caring.

Holy Name, January 1

C

Theme: Hallowed be thy Name.

Psalm 8

In the refrain with which this psalm opens and closes, God's Name is the revelation of his nature. The intervening verses expand on this, ringing with fear and joy, thus blending the two opposite fundamental religious attitudes.

Exodus 34:1-8

The background of this passage is the giving of the Ten Commandments, the impatient people worshipping the golden calf, and Moses breaking the tablets on which the Commandments were written (Exod.32). Now Moses goes up the mountain a second time to receive the Commandments from God. He proclaims the Name of the Lord in the words of the old liturgical confession which is often repeated throughout the O.T. (II Chron. 30:9; Neh. 9:17, 31; Joel 2:13; Jonah 4:2; Ps. 86:15; etc.). (Note: In v.5 most commentators designate Moses as the subject of the verb "stood." The reading becomes clearer if this is done.)

Romans 1:1-7

The salutation with which Paul's epistle opens indicates the motive which inspired his mission. Through Jesus Christ our Lord "we have received grace (power) and apostleship to bring about obedience to the faith for the sake of his name among all nations" (v.5). This passage lies behind Edward Perronet's hymn "All hail the power of Jesus' Name!"

Luke 2:15-21

This is the account of the naming of Jesus in the nativity story. The name Jesus means "Yahweh is salvation." He was given this name because "he will save his people from their sins" (Mt. 1:21).

Second Sunday after Christmas

C

Theme: Pilgrims all/The pilgrimage of God's people

Psalm 84 [at the Eucharist: vss. 1-8)

This is a pilgrim song. "Happy are the people. . . whose hearts are set on the pilgrims' way" (v.4). This could once have been sung by the Holy Family as they journeyed to the feast at Jerusalem or in essence been the sentiment of the Wise Men as they journeyed.

Jeremiah 31:7-14

Within Jeremiah's book is a little Book of Comfort (chaps. 30-31). This portion of it describes in a poem the return to Zion of exiles from all nations.

Ephesians 1:3-6, 15-19a

The writer begins his epistle with thanksgiving for the receipt of "every spiritual blessing in the heavenly places" (v.3) by the Ephesians, whom he describes as "having the eyes of your hearts enlightened" (v.18). They had made a spiritual pilgrimage.

Matthew 2:13-15, 19-23

This is the account of the flight of the Holy Family into Egypt to avoid the wrath of King Herod, and of their ultimate return to Galilee and the city of Nazareth, where Jesus grew up.

(Lead in: *"Now when the wise men departed from Herod's court, behold. . . . "*)

Alternate Gospel-Luke 2:41-52

The only boyhood story about Jesus is this account of what happened when he and his family made the pilgrimage to Jerusalem at Passover time.

(Lead in: *"Now Jesus' parents went. . . . "*)

Alternate Gospel-Matthew 2:1-12

The story of the Wise Men coming to worship the Christ Child is a beloved part of the Christmas sequence. The major theme of Matthew's Gospel is that the Jews rejected the offered salvation but the Gentiles accepted it. This story introduces that theme. While this reading anticipates the Feast of the Epiphany, where it properly belongs, it is also appropriate here, since the Wise Men were making a religious pilgrimage.

The Epiphany, January 6

C

Theme: All the earth will come and worship him.

Psalm 72 [at the Eucharist: vss. 1-2, 10-17]

Some scholars have interpreted this psalm as referring to the Messiah. Its appropriateness on this feast lies in the fact that the psalmist foresaw that kings of other lands would bow down before him (vss. 10-11, 15).

Isaiah 60: 1-6, 9

The prophet assures the Babylonian exiles that God will save and restore his people. This will be witnessed by the nations, who will therefore come and worship the Savior God. In effect, the passage puts into poetry the message of the story of the Wise Men.

Ephesians 3:1-12

The theme of this epistle is that all people find their unity in Christ. So the writer logically holds the conviction that "Gentiles are fellow heirs, members of the same body, and partakers of the promise in Christ Jesus through the gospel" (v.6).

Matthew 2:1-12

The story of the Wise Men sets forth the Epiphany message in picture pageantry: Christ is recognized by representatives of the nations who come to worship him.

First Sunday after the Epiphany

C

Theme: The baptism of Jesus

Psalm 89:1-29 [at the Eucharist: vss. 20-29)

This long psalm is a lament at the time of some great national disaster. The first of its three parts (vss. 1-18) is a hymn of praise to God. The opening section of part two (vss. 19-29) deals with the great promises made to King David. When we hear them on this day, we identify them with Jesus at the time of his baptism.

Isaiah 42:1-9

On the day on which we celebrate Jesus' baptism, this "servant poem" from Second Isaiah is most appropriate. Regardless of whom the poet had in mind, the Christian identifies the Lord's servant with Jesus. "He is my chosen, in whom my soul delights; I have put my spirit upon him" (v.1).

Acts 10:34-38

This is part of Peter's speech to Cornelius, a Roman centurion, and his family, all of whom were eager to be baptized. The good news he tells them about Jesus begins with the Lord's baptism by John and his being anointed with the Holy Spirit.

Luke 3:15-16, 21-22

Here is the event we celebrate on this day. The baptism of Jesus is a central Epiphany season theme. The active presence of the Holy Spirit in that event is described in terms of a voice from heaven and the descent of a dove.

Second Sunday after the Epiphany

C

Theme: The glory of the Lord is revealed and proclaimed.

Psalm 96 [at the Eucharist: vss. 1-10]
The Christian cannot turn back the clock and think of this psalm in pre-Christian terms. The good news of salvation which the psalmist exhorts us to proclaim to all nations and peoples is about Jesus Christ our Lord.

Isaiah 62:1-5
The glory of the Lord will be seen in the vindication of his once-disgraced and exiled people. And the evidence of God's favor toward them is described in terms of a marriage between God and his people. The Church is often called "the Bride of Christ."

I Corinthians 12:1-11
The Spirit was initially bestowed on those who believed in the risen Lord (John 20:19-20; Acts 2:1-4). In the life of the Church this same Spirit inspires members to serve acceptably, each using his particular ability.

John 2: 1-11
The account of the marriage in Cana has from early times been associated with the Epiphany season. It was one of the occasions when the glory of the Lord was revealed. The power of God is evident in unexpected ways and unexpected places.

Third Sunday after the Epiphany
C

Theme: Jesus fulfills Scripture.

Psalm 113
This family Passover song recognizes that the Lord whose "glory is above the heavens" is also concerned about seemingly insignificant happenings on earth. In Jesus this concept is dramatically evident: the afflicted, the brokenhearted, the prisoners, the poor, experienced his concern and loving kindness.

Nehemiah 8:2-10
Ezra the priest reads the Book of the Law to the people. They give rapt attention, and every effort is made to help them understand what they are hearing. It is this heritage of reverence for the Scriptures which caused the people of Israel to be called the People of the Book.

I Corinthians 12:12-27
This is Paul's classic pictorial description of the Church as the Body of Christ.

Luke 4:14-21

In Luke's chronology of the events of Jesus' life, this synagogue incident happened at the beginning of his public ministry. The good news of God's salvation, talked about by the prophets, was now being experienced by people in what Jesus said and did.

Fourth Sunday after the Epiphany

C

Theme: God watches over his witnesses.

Psalm 71:1-17 [at the Eucharist:1-6, 15-17]

This psalm is the lament of one who is threatened by malicious enemies. However, he has an abiding faith in God's power to save and protect him.

Jeremiah 1:4-10

This is known as "the call of Jeremiah." It is a description of his realization that he is destined to be God's spokesman. He is naturally reticent and afraid, but God reassures him. "Be not afraid. . .for I am with you to deliver you." Jeremiah learns that when God's word is honestly proclaimed it is a message of encouragement for some, and for others a word of condemnation.

I Corinthians 14:12b-20

Among the manifestations of the Spirit's operation in the company of believers was the ability to speak in "various kinds of tongues" and to interpret tongues (I Cor. 12:10). This practice had gotten out of hand in the Corinthian church; here Paul deals with the matter. Because there is a revived interest in speaking in tongues today, the apostle's words deserve a careful reading.

Luke 4:21-32

In the Nazareth synagogue, Jesus explained ancient Scripture in terms of the current situation. When his hearers realized that he was saying that familiar Scripture called them to account, they became angry. In their anger, they sought to destroy him who was both the messenger and the message.

(Lead in: *"Jesus began to say to those in the synagogue, 'Today. . . .' "*)

Fifth Sunday after the Epiphany

C

Theme: God's call is a challenge.

Psalm 85 [at the Eucharist: vss. 7-15]

This psalm has two parts: vss. 1-7 is a congregational intercession, which is broken in on by a single prophetic voice (vss. 8-13) foretelling salvation for the people. "I will harken to what the Lord God is saying" (v.8) is the attitude of heart and mind of those to whom God gives insight and a sense of mission.

Judges 6:11-24a

The Book of Judges is a series of independent accounts of prominent leaders of the tribes of Israel after they had settled in the land of Canaan. Gideon was one of them. This is the story of his dawning conviction that God wanted him to be a leader of his people.

I Corinthians 15:1-11

This is the earliest account we have of Christ's resurrection appearances—written about 55 A.D. (The earliest Gospel, Mark, was written about 70 A.D.).

Luke 5:1-11

This is an unsuspectedly difficult passage. Many scholars consider it a misplaced resurrection account. As such, it can best be understood alongside John 21:1-19. Because of the resurrection, Peter will henceforth catch men rather than fish. For him and for us, experience of the risen Lord lies behind Word and Sacraments and a sense of mission.

(Lead in: *"While the people pressed upon Jesus to hear. . . . "*)

Sixth Sunday after the Epiphany

C

Theme: The blessed of the Lord

Psalm 1

Here are two vignettes, like the comedy/tragedy masks which symbolize drama, giving a glimpse of the good and the bad.

Jeremiah 17:5-10

To the prophet, the blessed person is one who trusts in God's power. He pictures him as being like a tree growing near water in a desert land. Verses 7 and 8 are among the most beautiful and provocative in all this prophet's writing.

I Corinthians 15:12-20

The central issue for the Christian is the Lord's resurrection. If God did in truth raise Jesus from the dead, then God is stronger than all the combined evil forces of the world and is deserving of our uttermost confidence. If Christ did not rise, all else that the Christian claims to believe is of no consequence.

Luke 6:17-26

Luke's Sermon on the Plain (6:17-49) is an earlier, less stylized version of Matthew's Sermon on the Mount (5:1-7:29). The poor, hungry and persecuted who trust in God will one day be rewarded. The wealthy and the man-pleasing prophets who trust in human power and human approval will lose out in the long run.

(Lead in: *"Jesus came down with the twelve and stood. . . ."*]

Seventh Sunday after the Epiphany

C

Theme: The Christian and his enemies

Psalm 37:1-23 [at the Eucharist: vss. 3-10]

The psalmist seems to be a wise old person (v.26) who is giving counsel to someone who is upset over the prevalence of evil. His message is, "Do not fret yourself, be patient; your righteousness will win out, and evildoers will perish."

Genesis 45:3-11, 21-28

This is the emotional scene when Joseph, food administrator of Egypt, makes himself known to his brothers. Years before, they had sold him into slavery because they were jealous of him. In Joseph we see an awareness of God's watchful providence and of man's proper response.

I Corinthians 15:35-38, 42-50

Paul thinks through the logic of the Christian's belief in the resurrection. This is the central portion of his argument.

Luke 6:27-38

This is the portion of Jesus' Sermon on the Plain (6:17-49) which deals with the way a Christian treats others, especially his enemies. Here is the Golden Rule in context.

(Lead in: *"Jesus said, 'I say to you that hear. . . .' "*)

Eighth Sunday after the Epiphany

C

Theme: Hear and bear fruit that your souls may live.

Psalm 92 [at the Eucharist: vss. 1-5, 11-14]
   This thanksgiving hymn probably had a place in the New Year's festival celebration. The simile of planting and bearing fruit is a figure of speech used also by our Lord.

Jeremiah 7:1-7 [8-15]
   Jeremiah's "temple sermon" is a collection of his important messages and has been called "Jeremiah's Sermon on the Mount." Amend your ways, he says, and do those things that are acceptable to God.

I Corinthians 15:50-58
   Here is the exultant conclusion of Paul's chapter about the Lord's resurrection and ours. Because of Christ's rising again the Christian is assured that nothing, not even death or any supernatural power, can separate us from the love of God in Christ. Death has become impotent; its sting has been removed.

Luke 6:39-49
   This is the concluding part of Jesus' Sermon on the Plain (vss.17-49). In it he exhorts his hearers to "do what I tell you" (v.46). (Lead in: *"Jesus told the crowd this parable. . . ."*)

Last Sunday after the Epiphany

C

Theme: The transfiguration of Christ.

Psalm 99
   This is a hymn to the holiness of God. In the first strophe, God is praised for his world dominion (vss. 1-2), and then the congregation is exhorted to respond (v.3); in the second, God is praised for the establishment of righteousness (v.4), and again the congregation is exhorted to respond; finally, he is praised for his acts of grace and judgment in Israel's history (vss.6-8), and the congregation is once more exhorted to respond. The N.T. would add a fourth strophe about the cross and resurrection.

Exodus 34:29-35
   When Moses returned from having been face to face with God on Mount Sinai, his face shone with the reflected glory of the Lord. The passage might be thought of as an O.T. counterpart of the transfiguration.

I Corinthians 12:27-13:13
   Paul's great hymn describing and praising Christian love has long been associated with this last Sunday before Lent. It has nothing in particular to do with the transfiguration of Christ, which is now commemorated on this day.

Luke 9:28-36

At the transfiguration of Christ (as this incident is called), Peter and his companions realize that it is Jesus who fulfills their ancient religious heritage, symbolized by Moses and Elijah. It is the turning point in the Gospel. From this moment on, Jesus "set his face to go to Jerusalem" (9:51) and to the cross. In the coming season of Lent, we look forward to the cross.

(Lead in: *"Now about eight days after Jesus first predicted his passion and death he took. . . ."*)

First Sunday in Lent

C

Theme: A faith to live by/The Lord's temptations

Psalm 91 [at the Eucharist: vss. 9-15]

This mighty hymn of trust in God has appropriateness in connection with Jesus' wilderness experience. Satan quotes it in tempting Jesus (vss. 11-12). And the closing words of divine assurance (vss.14-16) seem to address themselves to that temptation scene although Jesus does not quote them. Actually, this psam developed in the worshipping community which knew of God's merciful goodness to his people.

Deuteronomy 26:[1-4] 5-11

Israel's faith was grounded in history. This passage, used as part of formal, liturgical worship, contains what might be considered Israel's creed. It outlines Israel's salvation history—what God, the gracious deliverer, had done for her.

(Lead in for v.1 or v.5: *"Moses said. . . ."*)

Romans 10:[5-8a] 8b-13

Biblical religion is spoken religion. Paul makes it clear that he who is faithful to Jesus Christ "believes with his heart and. . . confesses with his lips" (v.10). This practice had characterized Israel's faith from the earliest days, as the Deuteronomic creed makes clear.

Luke 4:1-13

Our Lord's temptations in the wilderness are associated with the beginning of Lent. Notice that his defense against temptation lay in his familiarity with the Scriptures of his people. His quotations all come from Deuteronomy, which sets faith solidly in the context of God's actions during the history of Israel.

Second Sunday in Lent

C

Theme: God's covenant with his people/Killing the prophets

Psalm 27 [at the Eucharist: vss. 10-18]
Here are two psalms in one: vss. 1-8 is a hymn of faith, and vss. 9-17 is the prayer of one in need of help. Because of God's covenant with his people, no matter what befalls they can say with the psalmist, "Await the Lord's pleasure; be strong, and he shall comfort your heart" (v.18).

Genesis 15:1-12, 17-18
Biblical faith is grounded in the covenant God made with Abraham. Out of this faith flows the developing insight as to the nature of God and the resulting religious practice and ethical behavior.

Philippians 3:17-4:1
The N.T. is the record of a new covenant relationship with God which fulfills the old. It centers in Jesus Christ, the crucified and risen Lord. Paul succinctly describes this loyalty and its demands with the declaration, "Our citizenship is in heaven" (v.20).

Luke 13:[22-30] 31-35
Jesus explains to his followers how hard it is for people to move from the old covenant with God to the new. In the end, those whom God sends to show the way—first the prophets and now the Messiah—are killed.

Third Sunday in Lent

C

Theme: The compassionate Savior-God/Divine forbearance has a limit.

Psalm 103 [at the Eucharist: vss.1-11]
This jubilant psalm in praise of God's fatherly love is one of the finest in the Psalter. God has revealed himself as compassionate and merciful (v.8), executing "judgment for all who are oppressed" (v.6); he does not deal with his people according to their sins (v.10).

Exodus 3:1-15
The call of Moses is a fundamental and pivotal event in Israel's history. On that occasion, Moses came to know that the God of his fathers cared about that pitiful horde of slaves in Egypt and, using him as their leader, intended to deliver them.

I Corinthians 10:1-13
Christianity is grounded in its Hebraic heritage. We are all "baptized into Moses" (v.2). The God of our fathers was first clearly known as the

God who delivers us because he had brought his chosen people out of Egypt. What he did in history gave the word "savior" meaning and prepared the way for the coming of Jesus Christ, the Savior of the world.

Luke 13:1-9

The parable of the vineyard is saying that God is patient with us, but that there is an end to his patience. That which he has chosen and planted in his vineyard has a responsibility to produce (cf.Ps. 80:8; Mt. 7:17-20).

Fourth Sunday in Lent

C

Theme: The Passover of promise and fulfillment/Reconciled to God

Psalm 34 (at the Eucharist: vss. 1-8)

This thanksgiving psalm has from early times been associated with the Lord's Supper because of the words, "Taste and see that the Lord is good" (v.8). It turns our minds also to the manna from heaven and the Passover meal.

Joshua [4:19-24] 5:9-12

A milestone in Israel's saga of salvation was entering the Promised Land. The people had come home. No longer did they eat the manna of wayfarers in the wilderness; now they ate the fruit of the land. Now also, the Passover took on deeper significance.

II Corinthians 5:17-21

Those who belong to Christ are a new creation (a new beginning). They start all over again, as did the Israelites who had just entered the Promised Land. This passage is the most significant description of the meaning of reconciliation in all of the epistles.

Luke 15:11-32

In the parable of the prodigal son, reconciliation takes on flesh and blood; through reconciliation the prodigal is able to begin life all over again on an entirely new basis. So it is also with those who belong to Christ (II Cor. 5:17).

(Lead in: *Jesus said, 'There was a man. . . .' "*)

Fifth Sunday in Lent

C

Theme: The water of grace/The inheritance of his suffering

Psalm 126
This psalm has been called "a precious stone in a simple and yet worthy setting" (Weiser). Originally it may have expressed the religious community's expectation of salvation in a time of adversity. The miracle of God's power to save is seen in terms of water in the wilderness (v.5), the greatest of blessings to a desert people.

Isaiah 43:16-21
To a nomadic people, water is life itself. God had not only chosen Israel as his own people; he was also the source of their life. That conviction lies behind this reading, which is part of a longer poem concerning Israel's redemption by grace (43:14-44:5). It might be called "Give my chosen drink."

Philippians 3:8-14
"Christ Jesus had made me his own," (v.12) writes Paul. His new life in Christ was contingent upon his sharing in the Lord's sufferings. Only thus does the power of his resurrection become real.

Luke 20:9-19
Jesus' parable of the tenants is a warning to the leaders of Israel and also a prediction of his own suffering and death.

Sunday of the Passion (Palm Sunday)

C

Theme: The passion of Jesus Christ

Psalm 22:1-21 [at the Eucharist: vss.1-11]
The prayer of a lonely, put-upon individual opens with those familiar words quoted by Jesus during his desolate hours on the cross. The similarity between the sufferings of Jesus and those of the psalmist is striking.

Isaiah 45:21-25
These several stanzas are from a poem (vss. 14-25) concerning the conversation of the nations. In them, God makes clear that he, the righteous God and Savior of "all the ends of the earth," will triumph.
(Lead in: *"Thus says the Lord, 'Declare and present. . . .' "*)

Alternate reading: Isaiah 52:13-53:12
This last of the four "servant of the Lord" poems scattered through Isaiah from chapters 42 to 53 describes one who humbly accepts suffering on behalf of his people. Scholars do not agree as to whether the servant is an individual, a dedicated remnant of the people, or the nation of Israel as a

whole. In any case, we think of this passage as one of the spiritual high points of the O.T. and see in it a description of the meaning of Christ's passion.

Philippians 2:5-11
Here in a nutshell is Paul's belief about Jesus Christ. He who humbled himself to become a man and to die on the cross is the Lord of all.

Luke [22:39-71] 23:1-49 [50-56]
The passion and death of Jesus Christ.

Easter Day

C

Theme: Christ is risen

Psalm 118:14-29 [at the Eucharist: vss.14-17, 22-24]
This psalm is "a powerful testimony to the strength of faith that flows from the direct experience of the help of God" (Weiser). After the introduction, there is the thanksgiving of an individual (vss.5-21). The portion of this section which we read sounds like the thanksgiving of the risen Lord himself (vss. 18, 22). The latter part of the psalm (vss.22-29) is the chorus of pilgrims attending the feast. Read on this day, it is an appropriate Easter hymn.

Acts 10:34-43
Peter was the leader of the Twelve and the first to see the risen Lord (Lk. 24:34). Here is part of one of his early sermons in which it is obvious that the resurrection of Christ is of crucial importance.

Alternate First Reading: Isaiah 51:9-11
This is a stanza of a poem on "the coming salvation" (51:1-16). On this day, when the poet speaks of the joy of the redeemed of the Lord we naturally think of believers in the risen Lord.

Colossians 3:1-4
The conviction that the risen Lord has conquered both sin and death is meant to influence all that the Christian is and does.

Alternate to the Epistle: Acts 10:34-43. [see above]

Luke 24:1-10

Each of the four Gospel versions of the events of the first Easter morning differ somewhat in their details. All of them agree that the tomb was unquestionably the one in which Jesus was buried and that it was empty. There is no suggestion of foul play. In Matthew, the soldiers guarding the tomb actually are bribed to say the body had been stolen (Mt. 28:11-15). Thus, his enemies grudgingly recognize that a miracle has taken place.

Easter Evening

Theme: The risen Lord gives us a new life in him.

Psalm 114
This is a hymn in praise of God because of the exodus, which is the fundamental saving act of God in the O.T. The Lord's resurrection is the fundamental saving act of God in the new covenant.

Alternate psalm: Psalm 136
This litany psalm bears witness to God's perpetual grace in creation and in history. A major event in that history is the exodus from Egypt (vss.11-15), which is thought of as the O.T. counterpart to the resurrection.

Alternate psalm at the Eucharist: Psalm 118:14-17, 22-24
This psalm is a powerful testimony to the strength of faith. The portion read here sounds like a hymn of thanksgiving for the Lord's resurrection.

Acts 5:29a, 30-32
This is Peter's witness to the resurrection before the Sanhedrin.
(Lead in: *"Peter and the apostles answered the high priest and council in these words. . ."*)

Alternate first reading: Daniel 12:1-3
The Book of Daniel ends with visions of the last days. There will be a time of general resurrection and judgment. This insight is reflected in the N.T. (Jn. 5:29 and Acts 24:15). One of God's great gifts is suggested here; the life that God has given each of us is precious, and he cares how we use it.
(Lead in: *"The Lord said to Daniel, 'At that time. . . .' "*)

I Corinthians 5:6b-8
Leaven has an infectious quality and was usually considered a symbol of defilement. But it was also the sign of a new start since its use meant that there was no sour dough left from a previous baking. In the Passover ritual, unleavened bread was associated with the remembrance of Israel's redemption from Egypt—a people's new start. Here Paul transfers that ancient association to Christ's resurrection and the new start which is ours because of the risen Christ.

Alternate to the Epistle: Acts 5:29a, 30-32 [see above]

Luke 24:13-35
Luke's Easter evening account is significant because the ways in which these disciples knew the risen Lord are ways which are ours also: the opening of the Scriptures and the breaking of bread—Word and Sacrament.

(Lead in: *"On that first Easter day two of Jesus' followers were going to a village. . . ."*)

Second Sunday of Easter

C

Theme: The risen and exalted Christ is the revealer of God's will.

Psalm 111
This festive hymn of praise is obviously appropriate for the Easter season. The Christian naturally thinks of these words in terms of the fact that God has raised Christ from the dead.

Alternate psalm: Psalm 118:19-24
On this day, these verses from the middle of a powerful hymn of faith are associated with the Easter event. (See Easter Day above for fuller analysis of Psalm 118).

Acts 5:12a, 17-22, 25-29
Almost from the beginning, the apostles' public statements about the resurrection of Christ caused them to be harrassed and arrested by the religious authorities. This is the account of what took place on one of those early occasions.

Alternate to the Acts reading: Job 42:1-6
The drama of the Book of Job closes with the hero's awareness of the omnipotence of God and his realization that God's purpose is never arbitrary or whimsical. In putting his discovery and his repentance into words, Job quietly recalls some of God's words to him earlier which he had not appreciated until now (v.3a, cf.38:2; and v.4, cf. 38:3). The wonderful purpose and almighty power of God is seen supremely in Christ's resurrection.

Revelation 1: [1-8] 9-19
In the initial vision of John, the seer imprisoned on the island of Patmos, the risen and exalted Christ (v.18) appears with a message to the churches.

Alternate to the Revelation reading: Acts 5:12a, 17-22, 25-29 [see above]

John 20:19-31
The earliest record of resurrection appearances is in I Corinthians

15:3-8. These fall into two categories. The first group (to Cephas or Peter *et al.*, vss.5-6) had a church-founding significance. The second group (to James *et al.*, vss.7-8) has a mission-inaugurating significance. The two appearances described in John 20 are in the first category. Jesus binds the disciples together in their conviction of his risen presence. The Holy Spirit is bestowed, and we have the beginning of the Church as a spiritual entity.

(Lead in: *On the evening of that first Easter day, the first day of the week. . . .*")

Third Sunday of Easter

C

Theme: The risen Christ is Lord of all.

Psalm 33 [*at the Eucharist: vss.1-11*]

This psalm is only related to the thinking of the day in a general way. The opening half of the psalm can be thought of as addressed to the risen and glorified Christ. When we read, "The Lord brings the will of the nations to naught; he thwarts the designs of the peoples" (v.10), the world concern and outreach of the Church come to mind.

Acts 9:1-19

Here is the account of the conversation of Paul. This encounter with the risen Christ was the pivotal experience of his life, which he must have recounted many times. Two accounts are on record: at the time of his arrest in Jerusalem (Acts 22:4-16) and in his defense before King Agrippa (Acts 26:9-18).

Alternate to the Acts reading: Jeremiah 32:36-41

At a time when Jerusalem was under siege and Jeremiah was in prison, he purchased a field in Anathoth, his home town, which was behind enemy lines. His dramatic act of faith in the future of his nation was coupled with this message from God renewing the ancient covenant. Here, in a sense, is a resurrection within history.

Revelation 5:6-14

In this heavenly vision, John, imprisoned on the island of Patmos, sees the risen and exalted Christ. He who rose from the dead is now the glorified Lord of Lords (see 1:18 and 19:16).

Alternate to the Revelation reading: Acts 9:1-19 [*see above*]

John 21:1-14

The crucifixion was disillusioning. The disciples were getting ready to return to their former way of life when the resurrected Christ came to them.

Note that the sacrament of loaves and fishes is shared with their risen Lord. The number 153 represents the total number of species of fish. The catch was symbolic of the successful universal mission of the Church.

Fourth Sunday of Easter

C

Theme: The Shepherd Lord has an everlasting concern for his sheep.

Psalm 100

This psalm, best known as *Jubilate Deo*, has as its keynote joy in the Lord, and it lifts the hearts of those who join in it. For us, knowing God's shepherd-like concern for his people is part of that joy.

Acts 13:15-16, 26-33 [34-39]

Paul and Barnabas, on their missionary travels, attended the synagogue in Antioch of Pisidia and Paul was invited to speak. The resurrection was always the central theme of his message.

(Lead in: *"Paul and Barnabas went into the synagogue at Antioch of Pisidia on the Sabbath day. After the reading of the law. . ."*)

Alternate to the Acts reading: Numbers 27:12-23

Joshua is appointed to succeed Moses as the leader of the Israelites. He will now be the shepherd who will lead them during the rest of their journey through the wilderness to the Promised Land.

Revelation 7:9-17

The Sunday-by-Sunday serial reading of Revelation continues with this vision of the glorified martyrs in heaven.

Alternate to the Revelation reading: Acts 13:15-16, 26-33 [34-39] [see above]

John 10:22-30

In this part of the Good Shepherd chapter of the Fourth Gospel, Jesus extends his shepherd concern for those who believe in him beyond this world: "I will give them eternal life, and they shall never perish" (v.28). The Shepherd Lord is the risen Lord, and those who believe in him will share in eternal life.

Fifth Sunday of Easter

C

Theme: God's Commandments

Psalm 145 [at the Eucharist: vss.1-9]

Throughout this psalm every mention of "the Lord" has something of the spirit of "m'Lord" for, as the psalmist makes clear in v.1, "God is my King." While God's graciousness, compassion, and love are repeatedly mentioned, his commandments are just off stage and are looked upon with no less trepidation and respect than that found in Psalms 19 and 119.

Acts 13:44-52

The resurrection preaching of Paul in the synagogue at Antioch of Pisidia was so popular that he and Barnabas were invited to speak again the next week. This passage tells what happened on that second occasion. Note that Paul considers "turning to the Gentiles" the Lord's command. Or put it another way: the fact that they were "Filled with . . . the Holy Spirit" (v.52) carried with it the implication that they were to be the Lord's witnesses "to the end of the earth" (1:8).

Alternate to the Acts reading: Leviticus 19:1-2, 9-18

This is the original context of the "Love your neighbor" commandment —the second commandment in Jesus' summary of the Law.

Revelation 19:1, 4-9

Among the visions of the downfall of "Babylon" (Rome) are two hymns of praise to God and the Lamb (Christ). The Bride of the Lamb is the Church, the company of those who are "true to the words of God" (v.9).

Alternate to the Revelation reading: Acts 13:44-52 [see above]

John 13:31-35

In his upper room discourses our Lord gives his disciples a new commandment which is more personal and more difficult to keep than the others, which we are sometimes tempted to generalize.

(Lead in: *"When Judas had gone out, Jesus said. . . ."*)

Sixth Sunday of Easter

C

Theme: The Lord is the giver of fruitful seasons/Christ's imminent departure and the promised Spirit

Psalm 67

This harvest-thanksgiving hymn would be more appropriate at the end of the growing season rather than at the time of planting. But in another sense, there is a seasonally fitting expectancy here. The opening verses (vss.1-2) are a prayer that God may come to his people. The coming of the promised Holy Spirit following the ascension answered this prayer.

Acts 14:8-18

This is the account of the visit of Paul and Barnabas to Lystra in the course of their missionary journey. The God-given power to those who have received the Spirit of the risen Christ evinces itself both in healing the cripple and in their spoken witness. Here on the eve of the Rogation Days, Paul's reference to God-given rain and fruitful seasons is most appropriate.

Alternate to the Acts reading: Joel 2:21-27

The people to whom the prophet addresses his message have suffered both drought and a plague of locusts. These words are a comforting prediction of better times. They also describe eloquently our set of mind during the Rogation Days as we ask God's blessing on our plantings.

(Lead in: *"The Lord said to his people, 'Fear not. . .' "*)

Revelation 21:22-22:5

The serial reading of the Book of Revelation continues with this vision of the new Jerusalem and of the new Garden of Eden with its river and the tree of life.

Alternate to the Revelation reading: Acts 14:8-18 [see above]

John 14:23-29

This portion of the Lord's upper-room disclosures fits well into our Christian-Year thinking as we stand near the eve of Ascension Day (next Thursday). Jesus prepares his followers for his departure and for the new relationship they will have with him through his risen presence, made manifest in the Holy Spirit or the Counselor.

(Lead in: *"Jesus said to Judas [not Iscariot], 'If a man. . . .' "*)

Seventh Sunday of Easter

C

Theme: Others believe because of the faithful.

Psalm 68:1-20

This is a complicated, involved psalm. It deals in part with the response of the praying community to the revelation of God. On this Sunday following the ascension, it seems especially appropriate because of such expressions as these: "Magnify him who rides upon the heavens" (v.4) and "You have gone up on high" (v.18).

Alternate psalm: Psalm 47

A part of the thinking about Christ's ascension is that he is enthroned in heaven and recognized as Lord of all. This is a major theme in Ascensiontide hymns. This psalm depicting the enthronement of God is quite appropriate. "God has gone up with a shout." He "sits upon his holy throne" and is "King of all the earth" (vss.5, 6, 8).

Acts 16:16-34

That which happened to Paul and Silas at Philippi made it possible for them to be the agents through whom the Roman jailer and his family became Christians.

(Lead in: "As we [Paul and his traveling companions] were going to the place. . . .")

Alternate to the Acts reading: I Samuel 12:19-24

This occurs at the end of the time of Samuel's leadership in Israel, just as his authority passes to Saul, the first king. The point of emphasis here is that God works through people's prayers as much as through their actions. Moses prayed for Israel (Num.14:20). Jesus prayed for Peter (Lk.22:32). Samuel will not neglect this responsibility.

Revelation 22:12-14, 16-17, 20

The serial reading of the Book of Revelation ends with this epilogue which concludes the seer's visions.

Alternate to the Revelation reading: Acts 16:16-34 [see above]

John 17:20-26

This is the concluding part of Jesus' high-priestly prayer offered shortly before his passion. He is praying for his disciples and for those who come to believe through them.

(Lead in: "As Jesus' prayer continued he said, 'I do not pray for. . . .' ")

Day of Pentecost

C

Theme: The coming of the Spirit

Psalm 104:25-37 [at the Eucharist: vss. 25, 28-31]

This whole psalm is a great hymn of faith jubilantly singing of God's fatherly love. Included in God's manifold works (v.25) is the fact that "You send forth your breath (or Spirit)" (v.31). The coming of the Spirit is what this day celebrates.

Alternate psalm at the Eucharist: Psalm 33:12-15, 18-22

This great psalm of praise is about God's providential rule from the beginning. Sending his Holy Spirit is evidence of his steadfast love.

Acts 2:1-11

The first Christian Pentecost occurred on the ancient Jewish feast of that name, fifty days after that Feast of the Passover during which the crucifixion took place. This day was the occasion on which the believers in the risen Lord first became aware of the presence of God's Spirit in their midst. Pentecost marked the beginning of the dynamic missionary life of the Christian Church.

Alternate first reading: Joel 2:28-32

The prophet sees in a natural disaster the prototype of the coming day of the Lord. In that day there will be an outpouring of the Spirit on all ages and classes of God's people. Wars and cosmic disturbances will warn of the coming final day, and, although that day will be fearful, the faithful in Jerusalem will be delivered.

(Lead in: *"The Lord said to his people, 'It shall come. . . .' "*)

I Corinthians 12:4-13

The gifts of the Spirit are various, and Paul seeks to make this clear, at the same time stressing that those varied gifts come from the same Spirit.

Alternate Epistle: Acts 2:1-11 [see above]

John 20:19-23

Here the risen Lord bestows his Holy Spirit on his disciples. In the Luke-Acts tradition this is a separate occasion from the resurrection (Acts 2:1-11).

(Lead in: *"On the evening of Easter day, the first day of the week. . . ."*)

Alternate Gospel: John 14:8-17

This part of Jesus' upper room discourse is appropriate on this feast because it throws light on the nature and function of the Holy Spirit.

Trinity Sunday: First Sunday after Pentecost

C

Theme: The majesty and holiness of God

Psalm 29

The psalmist sees the might and the glory of God in a storm.

Alternate to the psalm: Benedictus es, Domine [Canticle 2 or 13]

This is a hymn in praise of the God of Abraham, Isaac, and Jacob.

Isaiah 6:1-8

The sense of the holiness of God is a primary element in the call of Isaiah to be a prophet. No wonder that this prophet's favorite name for God was "the Holy One of Israel."

Revelation 4:1-11

This passage, along with Isaiah 6, conveys the awesome majesty and holiness of God. It is prose-poetry and should be heard and its meaning felt in somewhat the same way as one listens to great music.

John 16: [5-11] 12-15

The Fourth Gospel makes clear that Jesus is the sole possessor of the Holy Spirit (7:39) and that after the resurrection he gave the Spirit to his followers (20:22). God the Father, our Lord, and the Spirit are inseparably connected here (v.15). This close identity led in time to the doctrine of the Trinity.

(Lead in for both v.5 and v.12: *"Jesus said to them. . . ."*)

The Season after Pentecost

Directions for the use of the Propers which follow are on page vi of the Introduction.

Proper 1 (Closest to May 11)

C

Theme: The blessed of the Lord

Psalm 1

Here are two vignettes, like the comedy/tragedy masks which symbolize drama, giving a glimpse of the good person and the bad.

Jeremiah 17:5-10

To the prophet, the blessed person is one who trusts in God's power. He pictures him as being like a tree growing near water in a desert land. Verses 7 and 8 are among the most beautiful and provocative in all this prophet's writing.

I Corinthians 15:12-20

The central issue for the Christian is the Lord's resurrection. If God did in truth raise Jesus from the dead, then God is stronger than all the combined forces of evil in the world and is deserving of our uttermost confidence. If Christ did not rise, all else that the Christian claims to believe is of no consequence.

Luke 6:17-26

Luke's Sermon on the Plain (6:17-49) is an earlier, less stylized version of Matthew's Sermon on the Mount (5:1-7:29). The poor, hungry and persecuted who trust in God will one day be rewarded. The wealthy and the man-pleasing prophets who trust in human power and approval will in the long run lose out.

Proper 2 (Closest to May 18)

C

Theme: The Christian and his enemies

Psalm 37:1-23 [at the Eucharist: vss.3-10]
The psalmist seems to be a wise old person (v.26) who is giving counsel to someone who is upset over the prevalence of evil. His message is, "Do not fret yourself, be patient; your righteousness will win out, and evildoers will perish."

Genesis 45:3-11, 21-28
This is the emotional scene when Joseph, food administrator of Egypt, makes himself known to his brothers. Years before, they had sold him into slavery because they were jealous of him. In Joseph we see an awareness of God's watchful providence and of man's proper response.

I Corinthians 15:35-38, 42-50
Paul thinks through the logic of the Christian's belief in the resurrection. This is the central portion of his argument.

Luke 6:27-38
This is that portion of Jesus' Sermon on the Plain (6:17-49) which deals with the way a Christian treats others, especially his enemies. Here is the Golden Rule in context.

Proper 3 (Closest to May 25)

C

Theme: Hear and bear fruit that your souls may live.

Psalm 92 [at the Eucharist: vss.1-5, 11-14]
This thanksgiving hymn probably had a place in the New Year's festival celebration. The simile of planting and bearing fruit is a figure of speech used also by our Lord.

Jeremiah 7:1-7 [8-15]
Jeremiah's "temple sermon" is a collection of his important messages and has been called "Jeremiah's Sermon on the Mount." Amend your ways, he says, and do those things that are acceptable to God.

I Corinthians 15:50-58

Here is the exultant conclusion of Paul's chapter about the Lord's resurrection and ours. Because of Christ's rising again the Christian is assured that nothing, not even death or any supernatural power, can separate us from the love of God in Christ. Death has become impotent; its sting has been removed.

Luke 6:39-49

This is the concluding part of Jesus' Sermon on the Plain (vss.17-49). In it he exhorts his hearers to "do what I tell you" (v.46).

Proper 4 (Closest to June 1)

C

Theme: Under the authority of God

Psalm 96 [at the Eucharist: vss.1-9]

The joy of this psalm lies in the psalmist's faith that all nations are under the authority of God, who is the righteous judge of the whole earth (vss.12-13).

I Kings 8:22-23, 27-30, 41-43

This is an excerpt from King Solomon's prayer of dedication of the new temple in Jerusalem. He obviously knows himself to be under God's authority.

Galatians 1:1-10

Today we begin the seriatim reading of Paul's letter to the churches in Galatia, which will continue through the next five weeks.

Luke 7:1-10

The Roman centurion understood about authority. He was subject to authority and had subordinates who were under his command. He recognized that Jesus spoke with God's authority and was able to command the evil forces of this world.

(Lead in: *"After Jesus ended all. . . ."*)

Proper 5 (Closest to June 8)

C

Theme: The Lord is the giver of life

Psalm 30 [at the Eucharist: vss.1-6, 12-13]

Sickness brought this psalmist to the brink of the grave and caused him to think seriously about his relation to God.

I Kings 17:17-24

Wonder stories came to be associated with the memory of Elijah the prophet. We are inclined to think of him as an austere, severe man, but contemporaries also remembered him as one who brought warmth, life, joy, and the creative power of the God he so unerringly served.

(Lead in: *"The son of the widow of Zarephath, the mistress. . . ."*)

Galatians 1:11-24

This is one of the earliest and perhaps most authentic autobiographical glimpses Paul gives of himself.

Luke 7:11-17

Perhaps our creedal conviction that the Holy Spirit is "the Lord and giver of life" is in part grounded in events like this in the life of our Lord. Before his death on the cross, he evinced the life-giving power that was to mark the work of the Holy Spirit in the Church. It was this same Spirit "who spake by the Prophets" and acted through them.

(Lead in: *"Soon afterward Jesus went. . . ."*)

Proper 6 (Closest to June 15)

C

Theme: The forgiveness of God

Psalm 32 [at the Eucharist: vss. 1-8]

Here is the song of a forgiven sinner. He addresses his fellows in the community of believers whom he wishes to spare the bitter experience of his own struggle.

II Samuel 11:26-12:10, 13-15

This is probably the best known story of adultery in the Bible: David stealing the wife of Uriah the Hittite. Nathan the prophet dramatizes the blackness of David's lustful act. King David's immediate and sincere penitence is balanced by God's forgiveness, but there is also punishment.

Galatians 2:11-21

This is the third in the series of readings from the epistle. It is Paul's condemnation of the inconsistency of behavior on the part of Cephas (Peter) and the apostle's statement of how faith in Jesus Christ applies equally to Gentile as well as Jew.

Luke 7:36-50

This is one of the occasions on which Jesus encounters a woman of the streets. Jesus makes it clear that adultery is a violation of God's law and not to be condoned. However, gentle forgiveness characterizes his attitude toward her, rather than harsh condemnation like that of the prophet Nathan in his confrontation of David (II Sam. 11:26ff.).

(Lead in: *"One of the Pharisees asked Jesus to eat. . ."*)

Proper 7 (Closest to June 22)

C

Theme: The majesty and protection of God/Him whom they have pierced

Psalm 63:1-8
The piety of the psalms is well illustrated here. In his intimate communion with God the psalmist is aware of the divine majesty (v.2) and protection (v.8).

Zechariah 12:8-10; 13:1
This is part of an oracle foretelling the victory of the Lord's people over the heathen in the day of the coming messianic king. The nation is under God's protection and is given his commanding strength. The words "when they look on him whom they have pierced" (v.10) may refer to a martyred prophet of the future or even to a martyred messiah. We naturally think of Jesus.
(Lead in: " *'On that day,' says the Lord, 'I will put. . . .'* ")

Galatians 3:23-29
Paul speaks of the transition from seeking to win God's favor through observance of the law and discovering that we have God's favor through faith in Jesus Christ. With this discovery, we realize both our divine sonship and our oneness in Christ.

Luke 9:18-24
This is a watershed moment in the lives of the disciples of Jesus. Peter puts the insight of the disciples into words: Jesus is not merely a prophet; he is the Messiah. To this momentous revelation Jesus adds another: he will be rejected and suffer and be killed and rise again. The majesty of the Messiah will be revealed through his death and resurrection.
(Lead in: *"Now it happened that as Jesus was. . . ."*)

Proper 8 (Closest to June 29)

C

Theme: The claims of discipleship

Psalm 16 [at the Eucharist: vss. 5-11]
In many ways this is a disciple's psalm: "You are my Lord, my good above all other" (v.1).

I Kings 19:15-16, 19-21
Elijah the prophet is told to appoint Elisha to succeed him.

Galatians 5:1, 13-25
The apostle lists and contrasts the qualities of life that distinguish those imbued with and motivated by the Spirit of the risen Lord and those who are not. Notice that the "fruit of the Spirit" unites people and builds up brotherhood; the other list is of behavior that is entirely disruptive.

Luke 9:51-62
In the O.T. law one could carry out the normal acts of filial piety to one's parents, but in the Gospels a person "must be prepared to sacrifice security, duty, and affection, if he is to respond to the call of the kingdom, a call so urgent and imperative that all other loyalties must give way before it" (Caird, *Luke*).

Proper 9 (Closest to July 6)

C

Theme: The coming of the Lord brings comfort and judgment.

Psalm 66 [at the Eucharist: vss. 1-8]
This psalm falls into two parts. The first is a congregational festal hymn recounting God's miraculous saving deeds (vss. 1-13); in the second an individual tells the congregation how his prayer was answered (14-18).

Isaiah 66:10-16
Second Isaiah closes with poetry depicting the new birth of Zion and the fire of judgment. Here prosperity and comfort are picturesquely described, but there is also an ever-present awareness of the facts that the Lord's coming involves judgment.
(Lead in: *"Thus says the Lord, 'Rejoice. . . .' "*)

Galatians 6: [1-10] 14-18
In the closing chapter of this epistle, Paul again emphasizes his conviction that to be a Christian means to identify one's self with the crucified and risen Lord (vss. 14, 17; cf. 2:20).

Luke 10:1-12, 16-20
Midway in his ministry, Jesus sends out teams of disciples to prepare people for his coming. His coming was to be and still is a time of comfort and peace—and judgment.

Proper 10 (Closest to July 13)   **C**
Theme: Be open to God's word.

Psalm 25 [at the Eucharist:vss.3-9]
   The psalmist is a pensive, honest soul. "Show me your ways, O Lord, and teach me your paths" (v.3, also vss.7-8).

Deuteronomy 30:9-14
   Think of the Book of Deuteronomy as a series of Moses' addresses to the Israelites. Here he is exhorting them to keep the Commandments.
   (Lead in: *"Moses said, 'When all these. . . .' "*)

Colossians 1:1-14
   This epistle opens with a thanksgiving and a prayer of supplication for the members of the church at Colossae. In some of his epistles, Paul is stern and firm in rebuking behavior. Here he is warm and tender. Paul, the good pastor, is loving and cares deeply for those he has brought into the brotherhood of Christians.

Luke 10:25-37
   The setting of the parable of the Good Samaritan is the lawyer's question, which implies that with all of his learning he does not know what he should be doing. Jesus' parable unforgettably dramatizes what Moses had stated centuries before: "The word is very near you; it is in your mouth and in your heart, so that you can do it" (Deut. 30:14).

Proper 11 (Closest to July 20)
                                                                                    C

Theme: The glory and wonder of things divine

Psalm 15
   The blameless life described here equips one to abide on God's holy hill, which is another way of saying to be able to appreciate the glory and wonder of things divine.

Genesis 18:1-10a [10b-14]
   God promised Abraham that his descendants would be "a multitude of nations" (Gen. 15:5 and 17:5). Here that promise begins to be fulfilled. The contrast between Abraham and Sarah is that he believed in the glory and wonder of divine possibilities while she did not.
   (Lead in: *"The Lord appeared to Abraham by the oaks. . . ."*)

Colossians 1:21-29
   Paul tells his readers something of his attitude toward the apostolic ministry and his part in it.

Luke 10:38-42

Here is a relaxed picture of Jesus in the home of intimate friends. Martha is preoccupied with the busy-ness of everyday affairs and misses the spiritual dimension of life which Mary received from Jesus. Martha, like Sarah (Abraham's wife), could not see beyond daily tasks and daily abilities. Mary had eyes to see the glory and wonder of things divine.

Proper 12 (Closest to July 27)

C

Theme: Be persistent in prayer.

Psalm 138

This is a psalm of thanksgiving offered because God has answered the poet's prayer (v.3). The conviction of God's loving concern for him stems from that experience.

Genesis 18:20-33

The writer had a sense of humor. Abraham's attempt to strike a bargain with God sounds like someone haggling in the market place. The point is that the story reflects a realization that the Lord cares for the individual and that the individual is not lost in the crowd.

Colossians 2:6-15

The serial reading of this epistle continues. Here Paul makes it clear that the vital center of the Christian's life is the victorious Christ.

Luke 11:1-13

In the arrangement of Luke's Gospel, this is our Lord's primary teaching on prayer. A part of it is the parable of the friend at midnight (vss.5-8), with its quaint touch of humor. The details are incidental. God is not compared to an unwilling neighbor (or and unjust judge, 18:1-7), nor is his answer laid to selfish motives. The importance of persistence in prayer is the only point. If perseverance achieves its end in everyday human relationships, how much more in our relationships with God.

(Lead in: *"Jesus was praying. . . ."*)

Proper 13 (Closest to August 3)

C

Theme: Earthly treasure and heavenly treasure

Psalm 49 [at the Eucharist: vss.1-11]

The psalmist wrestles with the question of how earthly possessions are to be valued from the moral and religious point of view, and what one's attitude toward them should be in everyday life.

Ecclesiastes 1:12-14; 2:[1-7, 11] 18-23

"The Preacher," as this writer calls himself, has had worldly success in acquiring many things, but when he realizes that "the man who comes after me" will get all that he has acquired he gives over to despair and becomes cynical.

Colossians 3:[5-11] 12-17

Paul exhorts his Christian readers to "do all in the name of the Lord Jesus." The result for such persons is that character as well as conduct is transformed.

Luke 12:13-21

Jesus told the parable of the rich fool to those whose chief concern was amassing material possessions. This parable illustrates our Lord's words in the Sermon in the Mount (Mt. 6:19-21), "Do not lay up for yourselves treasures on earth. . .but lay up for yourselves treasure in heaven. . . ." (Lead in: *"One of the multitude said to Jesus, 'Teacher. . . .' "*)

Proper 14 (Closest to August 10)

C

Theme: Trust in the Lord.

Psalm 33 [at the Eucharist: vss. 12-15, 18-22]

This psalm is a festival hymn, as the opening verses make evident. The latter half gives a picture of the kind of trust in God to which we aspire: "The eye of the Lord is upon those who fear him. . .in his holy Name we put our trust" (vss. 18, 21).

Genesis 15:1-6

Abraham is called the father of the faithful (i.e., the faith-filled people) because over and over again he places unwavering confidence in God's word and his promises. This picturesque story is part of the heritage which earned him that title. Abraham believed the Lord and trusted him.

Hebrews 11:1-3 [4-7] 8-16

This great chapter on faith begins with a definition and then gives examples of faith in the lives of men and women down through a considerable portion of the O.T. The section read on this day deals with persons from Abel to Abraham.

Luke 12:32-40

In this chapter Luke has a number of sayings of Jesus on the responsibilities and privileges of discipleship. This portion deals with heavenly treasure and the importance of being alert and ready for the unexpected return of the Lord. "Believe the Lord and live accordingly" is a thread which connects this passage to the other readings today.

(Lead in: *"Jesus said, 'Fear not. . . .' "*)

Proper 15 (Closest to August 17)

C

Theme: The fire of divine judgment

Psalm 82

This psalm borrows heavily from mythology. It pictures a heavenly court scene in which lesser gods are called to account because they have not fulfilled their duty of executing justice among men, but have shaken the foundations of the moral order of the universe by their injustice and by showing partiality to the wicked.

Jeremiah 23:23-29

In Jeremiah's series of oracles concerning prophets we find these words. God is not to be treated casually as though he were either unimportant or weak. While we are likely to think upon God's kindlier attributes—love, compassion, mercy—Jeremiah makes clear that there is also a stern side. There is a consuming intensity which destroys like fire that which is not genuine, sincere, and faithful. The psalmist is more profound than we often think: "The fear of the Lord is the beginning of wisdom" (Ps. 111:10).

(Lead in: *"Thus says the Lord of hosts, 'I did not. . . .' "*)

Hebrews 12:1-7 [8-10] 11-14

This is one of the Bible's clearest discussions of God's sterner side. Discipline is inherent in sonship. Parental love apart from discipline is shallow pampering. Luther called God's wrath the underside of his love.

Luke 12:49-56

The fire of testing and the fire of judgment are continual Biblical themes. We have here a rare glimpse of the inner mind of Jesus which reveals an agonizing mixture of impatience and reluctance. John had prophesied the coming of one who would baptize with the fire of divine judgment (Lk. 3:16). Little did he realize that the Coming One might be the first to undergo that baptism. W.A. Percy has captured the essence of this truth in Hymn 437 (*The Hymnal 1940*).

(Lead in: *"Jesus said, 'I came to cast. . . .' "*)

Proper 16 (Closest to August 24)

Theme: The shaking of the foundations

Psalm 46
The strength and hope generated by profound trust in God are superbly expressed in this poem. Notice the repeated references to the shaking of the foundations of life (vss.2, 5, 6); but God "our stronghold" is "a very present help in trouble" (vss. 1, 11).

Isaiah 28:14-22
In this awesome oracle the prophet berates the rulers of Jerusalem because they have deliberately entered into a covenant to serve, in return for protection, the god of the underworld (Death) rather than the God of their fathers.

Hebrews 12:18-19, 22-29
These are obviously words of warning like those of an O.T. prophet. God will "shake not only the earth but also the heaven" (v.26). Those who have received the kingdom will survive; for others this will be their doom. Here is warning, but the dominant note is assurance.

Luke 13:22-30
The kingdom of God is entered by a narrow door through which one must thrust oneself with determination. It will not remain open indefinitely, and those who miss the present opportunity may find that they are too late. Throughout this passage Jesus is also saying that the standards of the heavenly kingdom are so different from those of earth that there are bound to be many surprises.

(Lead in: *"Jesus went on his way. . . ."*)

Proper 17 (Closest to August 31)

Theme: Be not proud/Be generous to the poor.

Psalm 112
This psalm sings of the blessedness of godliness. A major characteristic of "the man who fears the Lord" is that he is generous (vss. 5, 9). He is also "merciful and compassionate" (v.4)—traits which no arrogant person has.

Ecclesiasticus 10:[7-11] 12-18
"Arrogance is hateful before God and before men." "The beginning of pride is sin" (vss.7, 13).

Hebrews 13:1-8

This epistle closes with a series of personal admonitions. They tell us something of the level of behavior to which Christians aspired during the second generation of the Christian era.

Luke 14:1, 7-14

These are two parables Jesus told while a dinner guest in someone's home. One makes clear that, as in social etiquette so in the spiritual realm, recognition eludes those who demand it. This parable was inspired by the behavior of proud Pharisees. The second parable points out that heavenly blessedness comes to those who show hospitality and kindness where there is no possibility of recompense.

(Lead in: *"One sabbath when Jesus went to dine. . . ."*)

Proper 18 (Closest to September 7)

C

Theme: Choose you this day whom you will serve.

Psalm 1

This psalm opens with a beatitude—a word of comfort promising happiness to those who have made the choice of godliness.

Deuteronomy 30:15-20

This is the conclusion of Moses' third address to the Israelites, in which he discusses their covenant with God. He puts the decision up to them whether they will accept the covenant or not.

(Lead in: *"Moses said, 'See, I have set before. . . .' "*)

Philemon 1-20

This is the letter Paul gave to Onesimus, a runaway slave, who was voluntarily returning to his master, Philemon. It tells us something of the quality of life and relationships in the Christian community in the early days of the Church.

Luke 14: 25-33

The Semitic way of saying "I prefer this to that" is, "I like this and hate that." Thus, for the followers of Jesus to hate their families meant giving the family second place in their affections. Ties of kinship or any other ties must not be allowed to interfere with there absolute commitment to the kingdom.

(Lead in: *"Now great multitudes accompanied Jesus. . . ."*)

Proper 19 (Closest to September 14)

C

Theme: The merciful and forgiving God

Psalm 51:1-18 [at the Eucharist: vss.1-11]

This psalm contains the essence of true penitence. Here is the way in which one who is genuinely penitent comes into God's presence, seeking his mercy and forgiveness.

Exodus 32:1, 7-14

Intertwined with the account of the giving of the Ten Commandments is the story of the golden calf. This part of that story pictures Moses as the great intercessor. God has disowned the apostate Israelites. (He refers to them as "Moses' people," not "my people," v.7.) Moses pleads with God to be true to his character and his promise to Abraham. So God in effect reaffirms his commitment to be the merciful and forgiving father of his people.

I Timothy 1:12-17

This bit of biographical information about Paul makes it clear that the great work he ultimately did was possible because of God's mercy and forgiveness.

Luke 15:1-10

In his parables of the lost sheep and the lost coin, Jesus teaches that God is not only merciful and forgiving to those who have wilfully strayed, like sheep. He is equally concerned for those who are lost through no fault of their own, like coins.

Proper 20 (Closest to September 21)

C

Theme: Fear the Lord, but also seek him.

Psalm 138

A part of the cause of thanksgiving here is that the psalmist (in view of the fact that his prayer has been answered, v.3) is convinced that God cares about him and will keep him safe in the midst of trouble (vss.6-7).

Amos 8:4-7 [8-12]

Amos was a stern spokesman for God. As was said of Émile Zola, "He was the conscience of his people for a moment of time." These words are among his oracles. They deal with present iniquity and impending doom.

I Timothy 2:1-8

The writer stresses the importance of intercessory prayer and underscores his conviction of the universality of the Christian faith.

Luke 16:1-13

Jesus stood in the tradition of the prophets who knew that man's iniquity could not but provoke the judgment of God. This parable is one of warning. The point is that children of this world cope with an emergency in their temporal affairs with a far-sighted realism and acumen that religious folk might well copy in their pursuit of their religious calling.

(Lead in: *"Jesus said to his disciples. . . ."*)

Proper 21 (Closest to September 28)

C

Theme: Set your hope in the Lord, not in riches, and be compassionate.

Psalm 146 [at the Eucharist: vss. 4-9]

This is a simple hymn of trust. The psalmist sets his "hope in the Lord his God" (v.4), whom he knows to be compassionate to the oppressed, the homeless, and the defenseless.

Amos 6:1-7

Amos was a discomforting prophet. God as the God of justice loomed so large for him that all injustice had to be revealed for what it was and denounced in God's name. Here he condemns the blind pride which shuts the people off from God and the self-indulgence which insulates them from compassion for those in need.

I Timothy 6:11-19

Here is pastoral advice to a leader of the second generation Christian Church. Part of it (vss. 17-19) deals with the nature of true riches.

Luke 16:19-31

This parable teaches that the rich man's brothers were as he had been on earth. His mind had been closed to the revelation of God already available to him, and his heart had been closed to the demands of compassion.

Proper 22 (Closest to October 5)

C

Theme: Righteousness is a way of life/Live by faith.

Psalm 37:1-23 [at the Eucharist: vss. 3-10]

The psalmist seems to be a wise old person (v.26) who is counselling someone who is upset over the prevalence of evil. His advice is, "Do not fret yourself; be patient. Your righteousness will win out, and the evildoers will perish" (vss. 7, 10, 20).

Habakkuk 1:1-6 [7-11] 12-13; 2:1-4

Habakkuk, like many another righteous person, bombards heaven's gates with questions about the prevalence of violence, destruction, and injustice. He cannot understand why the Lord, "my Holy One," keeps silent and permits such things to continue. Then comes the Lord's answer: he who is not upright will fail, "but the righteous shall live by his faith" (2:2-4).

II Timothy 1: [1-5] 6-14

This little epistle, which we begin to read serially today, opens with an expression of the writer's confidence in Timothy as a minister, and then goes on to urge him to adhere to the teaching about Christ Jesus which he has received.

Luke 17:5-10

This passage is part of a longer section of Jesus' teaching on several subjects. In its opening verses the Lord says that faith in God is a power which takes impossibilities in its stride. This is followed by the parable of the master and the slave, which is a warning against a bookkeeping mentality in our relations with God. Therefore, abandon the idea of building up merit in your approach to God.

Proper 23 (Closest to October 12)

C

Theme: Gratitude for God's goodness

Psalm 113

Here is an expression of gratitude for God's gracious sovereignty which couples God's incomparable majesty with his wonderful compassion for those who are dispossessed by men.

Ruth 1:[1-7] 8-19a

The poignant story of Ruth is full of the gratitude of a foreigner.

II Timothy 2: [3-7] 8-15

The Sunday-by-Sunday reading of this epistle brings us to an older churchman's advice to his successor regarding being a minister of Christ.

Luke 17:11-19

The healing of the ten lepers results in the gratitude of one of them.
(Lead in: *"On the way to Jerusalem Jesus was. . . ."*)

Proper 24 (Closest to October 19)   C

Theme: Striving with the Lord.

Psalm 121

The quiet confidence of this psalm needs to lie behind all our relations with God. "From where is my help to come?. . .from the Lord." A person with this deep conviction is persistent in prayer.

Genesis 32:3-8, 22-30

This is the story of Jacob returning to his homeland after a long absence. Years earlier Jacob had received the blessing intended for his brother Esau and had left the country to avoid Esau's wrath. Now he returns, and a meeting with Esau is imminent. All of his life Jacob has gotten things by devious means. Now he wrestles in the darkness with a stranger and then learns that he has wrestled with God. Perhaps that wrestling was necessary before he was able to rely on God in his meeting with Esau.

II Timothy 3:14-4:5

The serial reading of this epistle continues with the author's comments on the inspiration of Scripture and his charge to Timothy to fulfill his ministry.

Luke 18:1-8a

In Jesus' parable on prayer the widow strove against an unscrupulous judge with no weapon but her persistence, and she prevailed. Our prayers need to have this same characteristic.

Proper 25 (Closest to October 26)

                                                                                 C

Theme: Confess your sins and trust in the Lord.

Psalm 84 [at the Eucharist: vss.1-6]

This is the song of pilgrims on their way to the temple at Jerusalem. The people whose strength is in the Lord are those who are honest about themselves and confess their sins. They have set their hearts on the pilgrim's way (v.4). Truly happy (or blessed or justified) are those who put their trust in the Lord (v.11).

Jeremiah 14:[1-6] 7-10, 19-22

It was a time of drought. The prophet recognizes it as divine punishment of the people for their sins. Along with reiterated confessions of sin, this passage also contains repeated professions of faith in God: "Leave us not." "Do not spurn us." "We set our hope on thee."

II Timothy 4:6-8, 16-18
Here are the dying words of one who has been a vigorous and faithful proclaimer of the Gospel.

Luke 18:9-14
The parable of the Pharisee and the tax collector is one of our Lord's best-known parables on prayer. The tax collector is "justified" in God's sight not because his is good and the Pharisee bad, but rather because he has faced the truth about himself and has cast himself on God's compassion. His approach to God is one of open-eyed honesty.

Proper 26 (Closest to November 2)

C

Theme: The forgiveness of the Lord.

Psalm 32 [at the Eucharist: vss. 1-8]
This song of thanksgiving is offered by one who has experienced God's forgiveness.

Isaiah 1:10-20
Isaiah's book opens with a series of oracles concerning the nation's wickedness—especially the people's religious insincerity and the irrelevance of their religious practices to daily life. The prophet exhorts the people to "cease to do evil, learn to do good" (vss. 16-17), and he holds out the possibility of forgiveness. This is an example of Isaiah's most telling poetry.

II Thessalonians 1:1-5 [6-10] 11-12
Paul's earliest epistles were to the church at Thessalonica (50-51 A.D.). This one opens with a prayer of thanksgiving and words of reassurance to that band of Christians who were undergoing persecution. Being a Christian is a serious, costly, and painful business requiring deep dedication. That is why Paul prays that "God may make you worthy of his call" (v.11).

Luke 19:1-10
Zacchaeus may have shown something more than idle curiosity in seeking to see Jesus. In any case, Jesus awakened in him a fine and generous spirit. His response to his encounter with Jesus was one of penitence and openness, which paved the way for salvation (wholeness and health in every respect) to come to him.

Proper 27 (Closest to November 9)

C

Theme: The Redeemer sustains us here and hereafter.

Psalm 17 [at the Eucharist: vss. 1-8]

The psalmist is falsely accused and friendless. Here he pleads for vindication. It appears that he believes in life beyond the grave (v.16), although this is not likely. However, his deep faith in God's ability to redeem him is unquestionable.

Job 19:23-27a

Job is in the depths of despair and loneliness. His appeal to his friends is of no avail (vs.21-22). Now he bursts forth with "the most momentous expression of faith which may be found in the poem and perhaps in the entire Hebrew Bible" (*The Interpreter's Bible*). The Hebrew is most emphatic: "I *know* that my Redeemer lives."

(Lead in: *"Job said, 'Oh, that my words. . . .' "*)

II Thessalonians 2:13-3:5

Paul is a true evangelist. This passage reflects his attitude toward his work and his successes. "God chose you from the beginning to be saved. . .he called you through our gospel. . .pray for us, that the word of the Lord may speed on and triumph" (2:13, 14; 3:1).

Luke 20:27 [28-33] 34-38

The Sadducees are here attempting to embarrass Jesus with a question about the hereafter. They did not believe in eternal life; Jesus, of course, did. He may have been saying that marriage, which is necessary on earth for the propagation of the race and for assuring legal succession, becomes irrelevant beyond the grave. At death whatever we may lose, we shall not lose God.

(Lead in: *"Then came to Jesus some. . . ."*)

Proper 28 (Closest to November 16)

C

Theme: Prepare for the coming day of the Lord.

Psalm 98 [at the Eucharist: vss. 5-10]

The Psalmist has utter faith in God's ruling power. His righteousness and justice will prevail (v.10) throughout the world.

Malachi 3:13-4:2a, 5-6

The ungodly see no good in serving God. Then, through his prophet, the

Lord speaks to the faithful about the coming day of retribution.

II Thessalonians 3:6-13

Here is Paul's work ethic. He was a hard worker and expected all Christian brethren to follow his example (cf. I Cor. 5:9-11).

Luke 21:5-19

Jesus foresees both a historic crisis within a generation and a final crisis at the end of history. Do not mistake the former for the latter, he says here, and beware of those who do. Like an O.T. prophet, he exhorts those who are loyal to him to be steadfast.

Proper 29 (Closest to November 23)

C

Theme: Christ the King comes to reign.

Psalm 46

This great hymn of faith in God is appropriate on this day because of the forecast that God will be exalted "among the nations. . .in all the earth" (v.10).

Jeremiah 23:1-6

The prophet speaks out against all the leaders of the people who have failed in their responsibilities. Then he foresees the day when God's Messiah will reign as king, executing justice and righteousness.

Colossians 1:12-20

Paul writes to the Christians in Colossae what he believes about all Christians: the Father "has delivered us from the dominion of darkness and transferred us to the kingdom of his beloved Son, in whom we have redemption, the forgiveness of sins" (vss.13-14).

Luke 23:35-43

The death of Jesus on the cross looks at first glance like the end. In truth, however, it marks the glorious beginning of his triumph and resurrection. Now he is the glorified Son of God. Christ is crucified: he mounts the cross to die—and to begin to reign.

(Lead in: *"The people stood by. . .scoffed at Jesus. . . ."*)

Alternate Gospel: Luke 19:29-38

The triumphal entry comes at the beginning of Holy Week. It has something of the flavor of a coronation. The King of Peace is riding to suffering and death, and those who shout as he passes do not yet know the profundity of their own words.

(Lead in: *"When Jesus drew near to. . . ."*)

Feast Days That Take Precedence of Sundays

All Sundays of the year are feasts of the Lord Jesus Christ. Only the following feasts of our Lord, appointed on fixed days, take precedence of a Sunday:

Christmas Day, December 25   The Presentation, February 2
The Holy Name, January 1   The Transfiguration, August 6
The Epiphany, January 6   All Saints' Day, November 1

All Saints' Day may always be observed on the Sunday following November 1, in addition to its observance on the fixed date.

Christmas Day, December 25
    Year A, see page 3
    Year B, see page 53
    Year C, see page 103

The Holy Name, January 1
    Year A, see page 6
    Year B, see page 56
    Year C, see page 106

The Epiphany, January 6
    Year A, see page 7
    Year B, see page 57
    Year C, see page 107

The Presentation of the Christ Child in the Temple, February 2

Theme: Dedication to the Lord/The presentation of the Christ child in the Temple

Psalm 84.[at the Eucharist: vss.1-6]
This psalm was associated with the occasion of a pilgrimage to the temple of Jerusalem.

Malachi 3:1-4
This passage is actually part of a section on God's justice and is usually associated in our thinking with John the Baptist. But because it speaks of "an offering. . .pleasing to the Lord" (v.4) we hear it on this feast.
(Lead in: *"Thus says the Lord, 'Behold, I send. . . .' "*)

Hebrews 2:14-18
This is the close of a section which gives a preview of the Lord's work of salvation. "He had to be made like his brethren in every respect" (v.17), so

his mother brought him to the temple to present him to the Lord as was the law regarding a firstborn male child.

Luke 2:22-40

Jesus was born into a devout Jewish family. Forty days after the birth of a firstborn male child, the mother brought the baby to the temple at Jerusalem "to present him to the Lord" (Lev. 12:2-4; Exod. 13:2,12). So Jesus, like other Jewish boys, was dedicated to God ("called holy to the Lord") at the age of forty days.

The Transfiguration of Christ, August 6

Theme: The revelation of God

Psalm 99 [at the Eucharist: vss. 5-9]

This three-stanza hymn to the holy God sets forth "the fundamental traits of the O.T. revelation of God" (Weiser). His holiness is praised because of his world dominion (vss. 1-3), because he has established righteousness (vss. 4-5), and because of his acts of grace and judgment in the history of Israel (vss. 6-9). On this day the O.T. revelation of God is seen alongside of the N.T. revelation in our Lord's transfiguration.

Exodus 34:29-35

When Moses returned from having been face to face with God on Mount Sinai, his face shone with the reflected glory of the Lord. The passage is a sort of O.T. counterpart of the transfiguration.

II Peter 1:13-21

Here is a reference in the writings of the early Church to the great event we celebrate on this day.

Luke 9:28-36

The transfiguration event is described four times in the N.T.: in each of the first three Gospels and in II Peter. It celebrates the disciples' realization that their Lord had fulfilled their ancient religious tradition, which in their vision was represented by Moses and Elijah.

(Lead in: *"Now about eight days after Jesus first predicted his passion and death he took. . . ."*)

All Saints' Day, November 1

Theme: The hosts of heaven

Psalm 149

On this occasion, the reference to the "children of Zion" brings to our minds the saints, known and unknown, for whom we are thankful to God. These are the ones in whom the Lord "takes pleasure" and whom he adorns with victory (v.4).

Ecclesiasticus 44:1-10, 13-14

In the wisdom literature of the Aprocrypha we find this paean listing those whom the wise old author thought should be remembered gratefully on an occasion like this.

Revelation 7:2-4, 9-17

Here is a prose-poetry picture of the seer's vision of the redeemed. Notice the contrast between their former lot on earth and the gentleness with which they are now treated.

Matthew 5:1-12

The Sermon on the Mount opens with these beatitudes, which describe those who have a place in the kingdom of heaven. Notice that they are not the famous, the gifted, and the accomplished by the world's standards. Rather they are the humble, the gentle, the innocent, the reconcilers, the concerned about others, and the persecuted. "The last shall be first, and the first last" (20:16).

Alternate set of All Saints' Day lections:

Theme: Where the saints have trod

Psalm 149

On this occasion, the reference to "the children of Zion" brings to our minds the saints, known and unknown, for whom we are thankful to God. These are the ones in whom the Lord "takes pleasure" and whom he adorns with victory (v.4).

Ecclesiasticus 2: [1-6] 7-11

Here is fatherly advice. It might also be thought of as a directive to those who would walk along the pathway which the saints have trod before them.

Ephesians 1: [11-14] 15-23

The writer prays for those who are taking seriously their Christian profession, that they may come into the spiritual riches which are "his glorious inheritance in the saints" (v.18).

Luke 6:20-26 [27-36]

This opening portion of Jesus' Sermon on the Plain is somewhat similar to (although interestingly different from) the Sermon on the Mount in

Matthew. Here Jesus describes those who belong to the kingdom of God. Luke's version is considered to be older and probably more nearly what Jesus actually said.

(Lead in: *"Jesus lifted up his eyes. . . ."*)

A

Angry with God 42
Ascended Lord both reigns and prays for us, The 26

B

Blessings: (*see* Gifts of God)
Baptism of Jesus, The 8; 58; 108

C

Call is a challenge, God's 110
Call of the Lord, The 59
Church, The:
  The people of God 10; 15
Comfort and judgment, The coming of the Lord brings 132
Commandments, God's: (*see also* Law, God's)
  God's commandments 72; 78; 122
  The Christian's view of God's commandments 12;29
Confess your sins and trust in the Lord 142
Covenant with his people, God's 115
Cross, The: (*see* Sacrifice)

D

Dedication:
  Beware of irresponsible leaders 46
  Choose you this day whom you will serve 138
  Decision—whom will you serve? 87
  Dedication to the Lord 146
  Good and bad shepherds 71
  Grow in the Lord 80
  Hear and bear fruit that your souls may live 112; 128
  The faith and commitment of those who belong to the Lord 64
  The price of righteousness 90
  The salt of the earth and the light of the world 11
Discipleship:
  Humbly repent and seek God's will 42
  The Christian and his enemies 112; 128
  The claims of discipleship 131
  The disciple must proclaim the news of his Lord 9

E

Evil: (*see* Sin)

F

Faith: (*see also* Trust)
  Live by faith 140
  A faith to live by 114
  The faith and commitment of those who belong to the Lord 64
  The importance of faith and works 31
Fear the Lord but also seek him 139
Forgiveness:
  Man's sin and God's grace 79
  Forgive that the Lord may be forgiving 41
  Divine forbearance has a limit 115
  The forgiveness of God 130
  The forgiving God is faithful 62
  The forgiveness of the Lord 143
  The Lord cares, forgives and heals 77
  The merciful and forgiving God 138
  The new heart of the forgiven penitent 66

G

Generous to the poor, Be 82; 137
Gifts of God:
  Forget not his benefits 62, 78
  God is a present help in trouble 61
  Healing and deliverance come from God 88
  Lepers are healed by the power of God 77
  The gifts of God 86
  The Lord is the giver of fruitful seasons 123
  The Lord is the giver of life 17; 129
  The mighty Lord has done great things for us 24
Glory and wonder of things divine, The 133
Glory of the Lord is revealed and proclaimed, The 108
God: (*see also* Forgiveness, Grace, Love, Mercy, Power, Truth, Word)
  One God—The Creator, Jesus, and His Spirit 28
  Man and woman in God's creative plan 91
  The majesty and holiness of God 126
  The majesty and protection of God 131
  The presence of the holy God 76

Appendix 2

Index of Bible Readings